Advance Praise for *The Conne*

"If you want to be a leader of the future, you must know how to build alliances and partnerships—*The Connector's Advantage* will help you do just that."

MARSHALL GOLDSMITH two-time Thinkers50 World's #1 Leadership Thinker

"In the new economy, it's not who knows you, it's who *trusts* you. When in doubt, don't forget Michelle's Law #10."

SETH GODIN author of *Linchpin*

"Too often I meet talented and highly skilled women who wait too long before enlisting allies who can help them grow in their careers. *The Connector's Advantage* is the book these women have been waiting for—a guide that clearly shows how to cultivate and grow the strong circle of connections that is key to sustainable success."

SALLY HELGESEN bestselling author of *How Women Rise*

"As a CEO and a leadership coach, I'm often called on to share my insights with others. My advice is always the same: create positive lasting memories with authentic, human connections within your organization and beyond. Not only does Michelle Tillis Lederman understand how to do this, but she communicates this knowledge with ease. *The Connector's Advantage* is the authoritative guidebook to navigating and maximizing the potential of your connections."

GARRY RIDGE president and CEO of WD-40 Company

"I know how many hurdles there can be to growing a business—a strong network gives you a leg up. *The Connector's Advantage* offers real, applicable advice on how to create authentic connections for reaching your potential, and standing out from the crowd."

DORIE CLARK adjunct professor at Duke University's Fuqua School of Business and author of *Stand Out Networking*

"*The Connector's Advantage* is a treasure trove of information about how to build strong, valuable ties that enhance your personal and professional life written by someone who has done the research and put it into practice."

DAVID BURKUS bestselling author *Friend of a Friend*

"There is no doubt that being a Connector is a huge business advantage and great step toward success. Read this book as a road map. Two huge Likeable thumbs up from me!"

DAVE KERPEN *New York Times*–bestselling author of *The Art of People*

"Michelle Tillis Lederman has the ability to drill down on human experiences and find the essential lessons to be learned from them. There are times I just want to hunker down with my laptop, but I add the most value when I'm out kissing frogs."

JOHN KATZMAN educational entrepreneur, founder of *The Princeton Review*, 2U, and The Noodle Companies

"If you've ever wondered why some people seem to be better at building stronger, more effective relationships than others, *The Connector's Advantage* is a must-read. Michelle Tillis Lederman is a networking virtuoso whose insights are indispensable for anyone seeking to take their personal and professional life to the next level."

JORDAN HARBINGER podcast host of *The Jordan Harbinger Show*

"Michelle Tillis Lederman's book, *The Connector's Advantage*, speaks to me in all the ways that shape the heart of my core beliefs about networking and building a connected support network. 'Connections matter,' Michelle says, and she couldn't be more right. Strategically speaking, nothing matters more. This book belongs in your top five business/leadership library. Keep it close—you will be rereading it often."

MAJOR GENERAL MARI K. EDER U.S. Army, retired, strategic communications expert

"Any successful businessperson will tell you that they didn't get where they are on their own. Michelle Tillis Lederman's book not only describes how to make successful connections, but also guides you through the steps of how to develop and supercharge the relationships that will take your life and career to the next level."

JEFFREY HAYZLETT prime time TV and podcast host, speaker, author, and part-time cowboy

"As a champion of promoting diverse and inclusive workforces, and empowering executive-level talent for people of color, my impact often depends on the quality of the relationships I am able to cultivate with others. Michelle Tillis Lederman's insights into creating, nurturing, and sustaining authentic connections are invaluable to my work in this realm. *The Connector's Advantage* has earned a coveted place on my bookshelf and will be recommended to the participants of our professional development academies."

VIOLA MAXWELL-THOMPSON president and CEO of Information Technology Senior Management Forum (ITSMF)

"When a networking guru like Michelle Tillis Lederman shares her knowledge, everyone should pay attention! The tools and insights offered in *The Connector's Advantage* are invaluable to anyone seeking create powerful, strategic connections in order to broaden their impact and influence."

DENISE BROSSEAU CEO of Thought Leadership Lab and author of *Ready to Be a Thought Leader?*

"Today, we can connect with people in many ways both digitally and in person, *The Connector's Advantage* explores the ways to authentically connect with others to improve our lives professionally and personally. In business, we need to remain connected in order to collaborate to solve the complex problems we encounter and need to solve quickly and innovatively."

RACHEL HORWITZ global learning and development director, M&M Mars

"One of the most powerful things an entrepreneur can do is create a network of authentic connections. *The Connector's Advantage* should be in every business-minded individual's library. Whatever stage your business or career is at, a carefully cultivated network can help move you up to the next level."

MATTHEW POLLARD podcast host, *The Introvert's Edge*

"Michelle Tillis Lederman has a black belt in networking and isn't afraid to use it! *Keeyaaa*! In *The Connector's Advantage,* she is your Sensei, teaching the moves and skills you need to become a master communicator. Full of 'judo chop' insights she has collected from other networking masters, it's a book no aspiring influencer should be without."

RYAN FOLAND keynote speaker and podcast host

"None of us goes through life alone, nor should we. Authentic, collaborative relationships are imperative to achieving any type of personal or professional transformation. *The Connector's Advantage* is essential reading for anyone desiring a stronger, more powerful launchpad for change."

LISEN STROMBERG author of *Work PAUSE Thrive*

"I've worked in the White House, Hollywood, and Silicon Valley—none of which would have been possible if I hadn't cultivated strong relationships with the right people. Like me, Michelle Tillis Lederman has walked the walk, and has the credentials to prove it. As one of *Forbes'* Top 25 Networkers, she is a virtuoso in creating connections. *The Connector's Advantage* is master class in networking, from one of the best."

JOHN CORCORAN creator of Smart Business Revolution

"We've all heard the saying: it's not *what* you know, it's *who* you know. It's also, as Michelle Tillis Lederman understands so well, how well they know you. As an HR executive, I can attest to the fact that the ability to engage and connect with others is a critical element of any successful career. *The Connector's Advantage* is overflowing with insights that will benefit individuals at any stage of their career."

RAVENA VALENTINE vice president, senior HR leader, people solutions at Cox Automotive

The Connector's Advantage

The Connector's Advantage

7 Mindsets to Grow
Your Influence and Impact

Michelle Tillis Lederman

Foreword by Ivan Misner

PAGE TWO BOOKS

Cataloguing in publication information is available from Library and Archives Canada.

ISBN 978-1-98902-535-2 (paperback)
ISBN 978-1-98902-536-9 (ebook)

Page Two Books
www.pagetwobooks.com
Cover concept by Katerina Ntelimpalta
Interior design by Setareh Ashrafologhalai
Editing by Kathryn O'Shea-Evans

Printed and bound in Canada by Friesens

19 20 21 22 23   5 4 3 2 1

Distributed in Canada by Raincoast Books
Distributed in the US and internationally by
Publishers Group West, a division of Ingram

www.michelletillislederman.com

For my husband, Michael,
You are the best connection I ever made.

And to my children, James and Noah,
You will be connected to me forever!

Contents

III. Diversify:
Expand the Way You Connect

Foreword

I FOUNDED what has become the world's largest networking organization, BNI (Business Network International, BNI.com). I'd like to tell you that I had the vision for an international business, but the truth is I needed some referrals for my consulting business. I put together a meeting of people I trusted and was willing to refer others to, and I hoped that they would be willing to refer me as well. From the start, I was a real believer in structure and system; we ensured no one in our group was in an overlapping business. When word got around about how effective our relationships were for growing our businesses, interest in our meetings grew. In 1985, we opened 20 chapters in the first year. Now we have more than a quarter million members in 8,000-plus chapters all across the globe.

I have learned a lot about networking, relationship building, and being a Connector. The philosophies, mindsets, and behaviors Michelle Tillis Lederman sets forth in this book align with the methodologies we teach every member of BNI. One of the earliest lessons I learned and now share is that networking isn't about hunting: it's about farming. Connecting means cultivating relationships and friendships for the long haul, not for immediate gratification and short-term wins. If you bring in people who embrace your core values, you will create an amazing network.

One of the guiding principles of BNI is *givers gain*. If you want to get business, you have to be willing to give business. You have to be there to help other people, and you have to do it openly, accepting that results may not be immediate. It is based on the age-old concept of "what goes around, comes around" and exemplifies the Connector mindsets of *abundant thinking*, *trust*, and *generous spirit* that you will read about in these pages.

What I have found over the years is that the most successful networkers share a few vital attributes. They are positive people who emit an aura of happiness. They are motivated to make good things happen in the world, and they have follow-through—when they get a referral, they actually pursue it. Great networkers tend to have extremely strong listening skills, and they're trustworthy. They are also open to meeting and working with all kinds of people, from the bottom to the top of the ladder—and with people who aren't even on the ladder at all. Diversity is key in building a powerful personal network, which is likely why Michelle dedicated the third part of the book to teaching you how to diversify your connections. The more that you surround yourself with people who are good at what they do, the more likely you are to get referrals. The truth is, networks are clusters. You never know who the people around you know. All of our work at BNI confirms this. BNI member referrals have generated $13.6 billion in revenue for member-owned businesses.

What I love so much about Michelle Tillis Lederman's book *The Connector's Advantage* is that she not only recognizes that these and other skills are requisite for creating a strong network, but she proves time and again that these attributes can be learned or improved. If you don't feel you're a social butterfly, don't worry: Michelle has solutions for you. If you're not very trusting, I'd wager that you'll be significantly more so after reading this book. Even if you don't feel you are a Connector now, you can become one, and all the knowledge you need to do so is within these pages. Givers gain—and Connectors gain too.

IVAN MISNER
Founder, BNI

Introduction

I AM not lucky. It is never my number they call as the winning raffle ticket and I've never even won $5 playing the lottery. Yet people frequently tell me I am lucky. They are wrong: I am not lucky, I am a Connector.

In 2001, I was working for a large consulting firm. Since people were always traveling, I did not think it was odd that I hadn't seen several friends from my start class in a while. I had heard a rumor about one being laid off but thought it was an isolated incident. Naive at the time, I was completely unaware that there had been three rounds of layoffs already when I was called in with dozens of others to the conference room one Monday in the summer of 2001.

I was stunned. I had never been laid off before. I thought I had been doing well, and my performance evaluations backed me up. But yet here I was, being escorted out with suspicious eyes watching me as I said goodbye to a few friends.

The next day, feeling a little more clearheaded, I called one of my best friends from business school, Dean, to share my not-so-wonderful news. His matter-of fact and immediate response was "Come work here."

Surprised and curious, I asked, "What would I do there?" Too busy to answer properly in the moment, he said, "Come to my office tomorrow." So I did. We chatted about school friends, significant and insignificant others, and eventually about what he needed help with at the large bank he worked for. Dean asked me to come back Thursday to meet his boss, Mark. I had no irons in the fire and no idea what I wanted to do next, but working on a trading floor seemed exciting. The next day after an hour-long conversation, Mark said, "Can you start tomorrow?" Speechless for the second time in one week, Dean stepped in and suggested I start Monday. And I did.

I hadn't been laid off a week, I was still receiving my salary, with a few weeks of severance to follow, and I just landed a long-term gig at a major bank. Luck? Nope. Connections.

I have a ton of stories like that one, and you will hear some of them in this book. But I am not the only one with stories of how everything just seemingly falls right into place. It happens to a lot of people— people who are Connectors.

If you are thinking you wish you were one of those people, you can be. That is what this book is all about. *The Connector's Advantage* is a follow-up to my first book, *The 11 Laws of Likability*. You don't have to read that book in order to understand this book. I will provide a quick summary in the first section to get you up to speed.

One step in the process of developing this book was doing the research. Working with a colleague at a local university, I leveraged validated questions to create a survey to test my assumptions about the attributes, behaviors, and mindset of a Connector. I received 742 responses from a diverse set of people, though unsurprisingly 82% of respondents self-identified as a Connector.

The majority of respondents, at nearly 83%, were from the U.S., though I received responses from 75% of the regions in the world. Women made up 65% of the respondents, and 80% had a college degree. The greatest diversity was in job title and field with respondents representing every job title option provided and 37 different industries.

The survey results were both expected and surprising at the same time and I will share specific findings throughout the book. While there was an increase in tendency toward certain characteristics in Connectors—such as high self-esteem and emotional intelligence— the overall differentiation was not huge. It was exciting to see that these characteristics were malleable. The good news is it is not just the way we are wired. Nurture can override nature and anyone can be a Connector! That is the point, connecting is accessible to all. My goals in writing this book are threefold. I want to demonstrate that:

1. Relationships and connecting are critical to your results, success, and your happiness.

2. Connectors have a way of thinking and acting that enables stronger relationships.

3. *Anyone* can infuse these mindsets and behaviors into their interactions and see the impact.

In working on this book, I talked about it. I told people my goals and my hope that anyone could adopt the mindset and infuse the actions of a Connector into their everyday to see the impact. When I shared, I also listened—and the responses were abundant! Friends and colleagues shared what they would want included, tools they would use, and tools they wanted to know more about. Then the light bulb turned on.

I started this book to share a perspective on connecting, and then it occurred to me: I am connected to a ton of people with expertise in building different types of relationships with different types of people and for different reasons. So I began to curate my connections to bring you broader expertise. Throughout the book, you will hear from many of my friends and expert colleagues whose perspective and knowledge enhances the thinking in and usefulness of this book.

I WROTE this book for you. If you are already networking, but all that effort is not translating into results. If you are just as smart, but everyone else is getting further ahead. If you are looking for a new job or are up for a promotion. If you have great ideas, but no one seems to be listening to them. If you see yourself in any of these situations, this book is for you! And even if you are already a Connector, this book will help you take it up a level.

I

What Is a Connector?: Why Connecting Matters

Connecting matters. Your relationships make the difference in the results you achieve, the impact you have, and the speed with which you make things happen. On top of all that, connections make you happier and healthier. The first section of this book backs up those claims. I present the concept of a Connector as a type of person. Almost everyone embodies some attributes of a Connector. Learn where you fall on the spectrum and determine where you strive to be.

1
Connections Are Critical to Success

"Just be nice, take genuine interest in the people you meet, and keep in touch with people you like. This will create a group of people who are invested in helping you because they know you and appreciate you."

GUY KAWASAKI

Real Relationships, Real Results

Real relationships, real results. That has been my motto and tagline since I started my business. I chose it because I wanted that to be the way I conducted and directed my business, not because I had any concrete knowledge that my way would work. It was simply my preference. And my business grew.

Regardless of your goal—a job, a promotion, a new business, or a referral—relationships lead to opportunities. And yet most of us let relationships fall into our lap. We rely on serendipity to meet the right people, and as a result, we miss out on an enormous amount of opportunities.

I think of it like this: in the agricultural age, the greatest asset was land. In the industrial age, it was the machine. In the information age, it became data and technology. **We are moving into the network age and our greatest assets are our relationships.** And it is not just the relationships we have as individuals. It is also the relationships we have with organizations—brands we love and trust and return to again and again.

The bottom line is that having connections helps you makes things happen. In this chapter, I'll share why the relationships we have and the connections we make matter so much to you—and to the organizations we work for and frequent.

My first book, *The 11 Laws of Likability*, was an attempt to explain my approach to starting my company, Executive Essentials, and to answer the frequently asked question, "How did I build my business?" I studied the drivers of likability and what enables connections to form. In this book, I am explaining the mindset of a Connector—a person who is people- and relationship-focused. I want you to know what I now know, the benefits of being a Connector. Beyond that, I want you to realize that anyone can infuse the mindsets and behaviors into their interactions and reap those same rewards.

What rewards am I talking about? Simply put, connecting and relationships will get you what you are working toward faster and more easily and often with an even better outcome. This book is an example of that. From one conversation with a connection, an introduction was made and a spark was lit. And this book became a curation of my connections and their expertise which, in my opinion, is a far better result than with only my perspective.

Faster, Easier, Better

My client, Cindy, has only been working for her current employer and in the New York area for six years. She told me that she had been living in the South, not far from where she grew up, and was ready to move. She reached out to a former manager and said, "I am looking for a new position—what have you got?" Within a week, he helped her line up several interviews within his bank and she had offers from multiple departments. Which did she take? The one working for her former boss, of course!

When you have someone to reach out to, or even the friend of a someone, the speed of your results is expedited. You are on the fast track. At Cindy's level, a job search in good economic times typically takes six months; in tough economic times, a job search like hers, at higher levels, can take up to one year. For Cindy, it took six weeks. She didn't need to go through online job boards, headhunters, or the human resources department. She went straight to the person who could make the decision to hire her. Her connection eliminated the gatekeepers and got her where she wanted to be, in New York, much faster and much more easily.

Fast and easy are great. The real magic of being a Connector is when the result exceeds what you were trying to accomplish. Kristen Lamoreaux, now the CEO of her own search firm Lamoreaux Search, used to fulfill that function internally for large real estate organizations. While an employee, she helped hire the CIO at her firm. He later left and joined an even larger firm in a similar role.

Kristen called him up to meet for lunch and told him, "I am thinking of going out on my own." She recalled the next sentence out of his mouth was "I have 14 searches; I'll give you all of them." And Lamoreaux Search was founded. Better than she could have ever expected.

Sounds too easy, right? The connection between them had already been established. Trust between them already existed, and trust expedites business. The connection continued, and so did the results for Kristen's business. He used Lamoreaux Search nonexclusively when he was seeking to fill a role. One time when Kristen called him, all she had to say was, "I have the person you need to meet." He said, "Great, don't send me the résumé now; just put it on the calendar." He ultimately hired that candidate.

Sometimes connections just save time but may not generate a result. I had wanted LinkedIn to get involved in this book and was connected to someone pretty high up. As a result of her inquiry on my behalf, I quickly learned that LinkedIn does not collaborate on books. That one connection saved me hours of effort trying to make something happen that wasn't going to happen.

Why Connections Matter to You

Take a moment and think about what results you are looking to gain from reading this book. What do you wish for in your life right now? The five most common responses to this question are:

1. "I want a promotion" or "I want to get the plum assignment." Along with these are responses about making partner and increasing sales or clients.

2. "I want to find a new job" or "I want to change careers."

3. "I'm starting a business." Related responses include growing an existing business, getting more business, and getting a business funded.

4. "I want to be happy" or "I want to be healthier." This often coincides with being more influential, listened to, and engaged in your work. Health responses relate to reduced stress, feeling more energy day to day, and living longer.

5. "I get it . . . I just want to expand my connections."

Is your goal on this list? Read on to learn how relationships can positively impact each one of these common responses and likely anything else you have on your wish list.

Promotions and Plum Assignments

A promotion is a goal of just about everyone at some point in their career. So how do you get promoted? The reality is, you get promoted when someone behind closed doors decides you deserve it. What you need is for someone at the table to be your champion. According to a recent study by LeanIn.org and McKinsey & Company, men are 30% more likely than women to be promoted to management roles.[1] One reason is that men get more chances to interact with top leadership. They develop the connections. Another study proved that over a five-year period, people with mentors were five times more likely to receive promotions than people without them.[2] The same tactic works for receiving plum assignments. At my first job, I was unhappy with the lack of follow-through on recruiting promises. I mentioned being disappointed that I wasn't working on the promised casino client to the senior manager who had recruited me. That was all it took. He made it happen and I was in the Bahamas working on a casino within a month.

If you don't have strong relationships with the higher-ups, develop them. Knock on the doors of your colleagues who have really interesting projects going on and ask if you can help them. If you simply let them know you're eager and available, they may think of you the next time they can use extra hands.

New Job

I have been following the statistics on what percentage of jobs come from networking for more than a decade. In the early 2000s, it was just over half the jobs at any level in a company. The U.S. Bureau of Labor Statistics reported double-digit growth over the years. The most recent study done in conjunction with LinkedIn revealed 85% of jobs come from who you know.[3] For those in executive-level positions, that number is likely even higher.

The numbers speak for themselves as to why relationships make getting a job faster and easier, and sometimes better too. I know people who have had jobs created for them because the people at the company wanted them, but there was no position that fit. You can't get a new job unless you hear about the opportunity. Often by the time a job is posted online, an internal candidate or a referral is already lined up for it. If you are in the market, put your feelers out like my client Cindy did. Use social media to connect. According to *Fast Company*, 79% of job seekers use social media in their job search. For those in the first 10 years of their career, this figure jumps to

86%.[4] Companies are using social media too. The more people you are connected to, the more likely you will come up in the employer's or recruiter's search.

My editor's husband recently found his new job—in a brand-new city, in a brand-new field—by networking. He reached out to people at all the companies he wanted to work for and politely asked for informational interviews. Within two months, after flying to the new city to take a few meetings face-to-face and prove how serious he was about moving, he had two job offers. It wouldn't have happened if he'd simply filled out an online job application and left it at that.

Start a Business

This dream I relate to—I have been there. To start a business, there are a variety of needs: funding, customers, referrals, and the basic knowledge of how to run your own business. All of these needs can be aided by your relationships. Funding is probably the highest hurdle, but the right relationships can at least get you the meeting. That's what Ari Horie, the founder of Women's Startup Lab (WomenStartupLab.com), intended to do for women entrepreneurs. According to PitchBook, female founders got only 2% of venture capital dollars in 2017.[5] Ari thought the reason women lose out is because they are not in a power circle and she wants to change that: "We become that platform to finally help them take off because what they were lacking is access to those networks." No surprise that Ari's approach is working. She has been able to help women entrepreneurs grow through the power of knowing the right people.

Relationships can get your business off the ground. People trust who and what they know. People also trust consensus and the opinions of people in a similar position to them, other consumers of a product or service. That is the power behind referral sites such as Yelp, Angie's List, and Rotten Tomatoes. According to Nielsen, people are four times more likely to buy when referred by a friend.[6] In a survey done by BNI of more than 3,000 businesspeople, more than half of the respondents said that they got 70% or more of their customers through referrals.[7] Nobel Prize–winning psychologist Daniel Kahneman has said that people would rather do business with a person they like and trust rather than someone they don't.[8] At the end of the day, the relationship often wins over a lower price and even over higher quality. People choose *who* they want to work with.

Happiness and Health

This may not seem an obvious answer to the question, "What results are you looking for?" But I would venture to guess that you wouldn't mind being a little happier and healthier, and connections can do that for you. This might not surprise you, especially if you're familiar with the world's longest study of adult life which began in 1938 at Harvard University, during the Great Depression. According to Dr. Robert Waldinger, a psychiatrist and director of the study, "Good Relationships Keep Us Happier and Healthier."[9] Humans are by nature tribal people, and quality face-to-face interactions and relationships truly matter to our emotional state.

Connection matters enormously to your overall health, even to your longevity. In a study of more than 3.4 million participants, Brigham Young University professor Julianne Holt-Lunstad found social isolation and loneliness to have a greater impact on mortality than obesity, and lacking social connections carries a risk similar to smoking up to 15 cigarettes a day. She found people with greater social connections were associated with a 50% lower risk of early death in contrast to people who were lonely.[10] The evidence tying your well-being to your connections is abundant. Research shows strong social connections strengthen your immune system, reduce stress hormones, and increase dopamine, which produces the sensation of pleasure.[11] Connections don't just feel good—they are good for us.

Relationships also impact our happiness on the job. According to the *Journal of Applied Psychology*, close work friendships boost employee satisfaction by 50% and predict happiness at work.[12] In its State of the American Workplace report, Gallup found that people with a best friend at work are seven times more likely to engage fully in their work.[13] Relationships even advance your impact and innovation. Research shows that the quantity and quality of your relationships predict how innovative you'll be; it has to do with the way your ideas meet and are transformed by others.[14] Per the *Journal of the Academy of Marketing,* when you are liked as an employee, you are seen as more trustworthy—and your ideas more credible. Happiness and engagement with your work is largely due to your relationship with your boss. A Towers Watson study revealed the number-one driver of employee engagement is the belief that management has an interest in your well-being.[15] I always say that to be a relationship-driven leader you simply need to show your employees two things: you care about them as people, and you care about the things they care about. Who wouldn't be happier with a boss like that?

Take It Up a Level

Many of you know this already. You have seen the power of relationships in your life and embrace the impact that being a Connector can have on your results. You don't need convincing; you just need to know how to take it up a level. You want to continue to expand your connections, nurture and strengthen your relationships, and solidify your designation as a Connector. This book will do that for you. Read on.

MINDSET MISSION
Connection before Content

Peter Block, an author and leader in organizational development, claims that, "We must establish a personal connection with each other. Connection before content. Without relatedness, no work can occur." Will Wise, author of *Ask Powerful Questions: Create Conversations that Matter* (WeAnd.me), shares a practical exercise to test the impact of being deliberate in creating connection before diving into content at the start of your next meeting.

Step 1: Formulate a single, powerful question to kick off the conversation. The question should connect people to each other and to the purpose of why you are there and create an opportunity for vulnerability.

Use the questioning techniques from the Law of Curiosity in *The 11 Laws of Likability*. Use open-ended questions that start with "how" or "what" and not "why" to reduce defensiveness and get people talking. One of Will's favorite questions is, "What are you intending to achieve and what about that is important?"

Step 2: Pose the question to the group and discuss for five minutes.

Step 3: Invite people to throw out responses to the large group to build a collective understanding. They suggest simply asking, "What struck you about those responses?"

This exercise allows people to connect before diving straight into content, learn about each other, and connect to the purpose of why they are there in under 10 minutes.

Why Connections Matter to Businesses

There's a very, very good reason why the popularity of Netflix soared right out of the gate—and it wasn't because people didn't have the energy to drive to Blockbuster for their TV-binging needs. It is because Netflix builds a personal-feeling relationship with its customers. It remembers what you watched, where you left off, and recommends other shows that you might enjoy. That's no accident: it's an example of the membership economy, and Robbie Kellman Baxter (PeninsulaStrategies.com) literally wrote the book on it.

Robbie found that organizations like Netflix, LinkedIn, Spotify, and Amazon have valuations that are 5 to 10 times that of their transactional counterparts because they've built *relationships* with their customers.[16] For them, membership is a mindset; it's about giving new customers value right away and continuing to provide value for the long term. She explains, "The companies that can tap into serving customer needs and building relationships will win." Many of those needs align with Maslow's hierarchy: the need to mitigate risk, feel a sense of belonging, and be recognized for your contributions. Proof positive that connections matter to customers: the subscription industry has been growing at 200% annually since 2011, according to the *Harvard Business Review*.[17]

It works in reverse too. A lack of relationship or poor customer-service experience results in the loss of business and repeat clientele. We all have those companies we'll never buy from again, based on how they treated us in the past or something that doesn't quite sit well with us in the present. For me, it's a certain cellphone company that, no matter what, I'll never do business with. It doesn't matter how good a plan or how great of a free phone they offer; the hours and hours of my life spent dealing with their less-than-pleasant customer service department is time I will never get back.

We have each experienced a business that tells you what it *can't* do for you. And likewise, we all know of shops that may be more expensive, but focus on what they *can* do for you. Some people have shared reasons for a company or product boycott far more significant than mine; they support a cause you disagree with, they test their products on animals, and some source their materials from regions that use child labor. Whatever the reason, the result is the same: a strong sense of unwillingness to interact or support their business in any way.

I know you are reading this thinking about a store or company that you feel this way about. Maybe you are reliving the experience and feeling fired up. On the flip side, there are likely companies that you absolutely love. I am pretty loyal to United Airlines, despite the reputation challenges they have faced. It started because of their hub being close to home, and the frequent flyer miles helped. But what really has me a fan is the experience I have when I call.

When I call from my phone number, they know without authentication who I am and pull up all my reservations. I called once trying to change my flight which I originally booked through a third-party website. Well, I didn't read the fine print and apparently my ticket did not allow any changes, not even for a fee. Without passing me along to the next person to say no, the customer service representative placed me on hold, spoke to her supervisor on my behalf, and came back and gave me the great news: I was getting home earlier and without being charged a fee! It is just the most recent example of how the airline has helped me navigate travel challenges. I don't have any status on the airline, yet they still help me. As a result, I always try to fly United.

If you are trying to figure out if you are a relationship-based business, think about your business model. Robbie describes two ends of the spectrum as handcuffs versus magnets. With handcuffs, a company forces you to stay with long-term contracts and penalties. These organizations build loyalty by locking people in. Magnets like Netflix are proud of the fact that even though members can cancel anytime, most of them choose to stay. Who do you think wins in the long run?

Trust Trumps All

Relationships are just as critical in the nonprofit world. According to a study done at Columbia University's teachers college, trust in the organization is the single biggest factor in determining if a person will donate. Trust level outweighed other factors—such as income, race, gender, education level, and the worthiness ascribed to a cause—as a predictor of their willingness to give.[18]

For anyone who has ever made an online purchase after reading five-star reviews, it is not surprising to know that 85% of people trust online reviews, based on the 2017 consumer review survey.[19] Trust is even stronger with a known source: 92% of consumers trust referrals from people they know.[20] It only takes reading between one and six online reviews for the majority of people to form an opinion about a product. Verified reviews allow potential consumers to get a sense of a company's trustworthiness and how they treat their customers. It makes it much easier to figure out which businesses to avoid, saving consumers time and hard-earned money, two very precious resources.

Great organizations are finding ways to build relationships and trust. Donors Choose (DonorsChoose.org) is a great example.

Charles Best, a former history teacher in the Bronx, was spending his own money on supplies for his students and figured there must be people out there willing to help. He founded the nonprofit, which allows the giver to decide which teacher's project they want to share their money with, based on whatever data they choose: their interests, passions, location, even the teacher's surname. What he found was that the transparency of knowing exactly to whom and where your donations were going increased giving manifold. The organization further reinforces the trust in the organization by doing the purchasing on behalf of the teachers. A donor never worries the money isn't making it to the students. Transparency leads to trust.

Relationships Impact Employees and Productivity

In their quest to build the perfect team, Google learned the number-one characteristic of a high-performing team was the degree of "psychological safety" in that team. The term was coined by Harvard Business School professor Amy Edmondson, meaning "a sense of confidence that the team will not embarrass, reject, or punish someone for speaking up. It describes a team climate characterized by interpersonal trust and mutual respect in which people are comfortable being themselves." [21] This trust is largely built and established through personal *connections*.

Rebecca Friese Rodskog, cofounder of FutureLeaderNow (Future LeaderNow.com), which consults on creating future-thinking workplace cultures, found a shift away from a hierarchy-centered organization—popular coming out of the Industrial Revolution and even into the '80s—to people-focused or networked organizations. "There's a recognition that work is no longer so discrete that you can just assign bits of the process to people and ask them to execute [it]," she shares. "Work is getting done through relationships and influence, and those individuals with the best relationships are getting the most work done and having the most success in their careers." She has discovered that organizations that cultivate relationships within their staff are the most productive and; frankly, considered better places to work, resulting in the ability to hire the best people with ease. Her client, Kronos, a 40-plus-year-old technology company, focused on people strategy and genuinely caring about those relationships. As a result, they found themselves on the Glassdoor Employees' Choice Awards Best Places to Work list for the first time in 2018. "One of the main tenets of their culture is people over process," she explains. "They value the connections and the support of each other over hierarchy and process and believe deeply that this is the key to their success." The data backs it up; according to research by the Temkin Group, 93% of engaged employees try their hardest at work.[22] Relationships result in a better bottom line.

MINDSET MISSION
Create a Culture of Connection

Michael Lee Stallard (MichaelLeeStallard.com) is an expert on how human connection in cultures affect the health and performance of individuals and organizations. In his bestselling book *Connection Culture*, Michael describes three types of cultures you need to be aware of and how each affect your health and performance.

1. **Culture of Control:** People with power, control, and influence rule over the rest.

2. **Culture of Indifference:** People are so busy with tasks that they don't take time to connect and build supportive relationships.

3. **Culture of Connection:** People feel a bond of connection to their supervisor, colleagues, organization, and its constituents.

Not surprisingly, cultures of control and indifference make people feel disconnected, left out, or lonely. These cultures drain the energy and enthusiasm out of its people. The connection culture benefits organizations by boosting employee engagement, strategic alignment, quality of decision-making, and innovation, and it therefore provides a performance advantage. According to Michael, a connection culture is created when leaders communicate an inspiring vision, value people, and give each person a voice. Michael provides ideas for each concept, vision, value, and voice so you can create and reap the rewards of a connection culture.

- **Vision:** Create a mission or values statement that makes people feel proud. The statement should be a guiding principle for internal and external interactions and decision-making. A great example is Costco's "Do the right thing." The company is consistently listed as one of the best large-company employers in America.

- **Value:** Value exists when people are treated as human beings and individuals. Leaders can show they value people by taking the time to get to know their team, their work history, and what helps them perform best. Find out their career goals and try to align their work so that it advances them toward their goals. Get to know their background and interests outside of work.

- **Voice:** Voice exists when the ideas and opinions of others are sought and considered before decisions are made. This reflects humility and honesty. Often the best ideas are from those closest to the work and the issues.

By communicating an inspiring vision, valuing people, and giving each person a voice, you too can bring out the best in people, individually and collectively, to accomplish great things.

WHETHER FOR personal reasons or to advance your career, connections undoubtedly make things happen faster, more easily, and often with a better outcome. This book itself is a testament to the power of connections, because it's filled with expert advice from my own network—and my network's network. Take Malcolm Gladwell, for example. I wanted to quote him and looked on various social media platforms, tweeted him, but got no reply. I thought about reaching out to his publicist or book publisher, but first I asked my trusted network and one of my contacts gave me his email. I reached out and he responded within a day. Rather than having to hunt high and low, I was able to go directly to him, thanks to my connections. This is what I mean when I say they make things happen faster, more easily, and often better. They do! And they can do the same for you.

Refresh
Your Memory

Connections makes things happen faster, more easily, and often give you a better result than without them.

Connecting is important to you because connections can help you get a promotion, plum assignment, or new job; 85% of jobs come from who you know.

Businesses need relationships. People are four times more likely to buy when referred by a friend.

Connected people are happier at work and beyond. Relationships advance your impact and innovation.

Trust is critical to organizations. Relationship-focused businesses, such as in the subscription industry, have been growing at 200% annually since 2011.

2

Likability Enables Connection

"Basically, likability comes down to creating positive emotional experiences in others... When you make others feel good, they tend to gravitate to you."

TIM SANDERS

LIKABILITY AND CONNECTION are, well, connected. Likability enables connection and is often the foundation for lasting connections. In my book *The 11 Laws of Likability*, I delved into ways to fully engage the power of likability, illuminating what it is and how it works. We are all, obviously, different, and that's a fact to be celebrated and embraced. What makes each of us likable is distinct to us. But the basic drivers of likability are the same for everyone, and that's what my book discovered. It gives an in-depth look at each of the 11 "laws" of likability, breaking them down to show how they function in both business and social settings and how to fully incorporate them into your life.

Because likability and connection are intrinsically linked, I provide a summary of need-to-know background on each law of likability below. If you want to read further, you can pick up a copy of the book, but it's by no means necessary. With the exception of the stories told, everything you need to know to understand the references to likability and connection made in this book is included in this chapter. If you've recently read *The 11 Laws of Likability*, you may choose to jump to chapter 3.

The 11 Laws of Likability

1. **The Law of Authenticity:** *The Real You Is the Best You*

   Authenticity is who you are—your honest reactions, your natural energy. Sharing what is real about you is the key to building real relationships with others. When you show your authentic self, people will respond in kind, which lays the bedrock for mutual understanding, connections, and growth. The Law of Authenticity is about being your true self. Authenticity is about being your natural self both to yourself and to others. It is woven into all of the other laws and it is the keystone to likability—the most essential tool for forming real connections.

   - **Be Your True Self:** The "right" way to be is what feels right for you, whether that's leaving an event early or staying all night, being the life of the party or mingling in smaller groups. Do what feels authentic, and people will respond positively.

   - **Make the Connections You Want to Make:** The relationships you genuinely care about are the ones that will form the strongest network you can build.

   - **Do It, Reframe It, or Delete It:** Understand your choices and adjust your attitudes to reflect your authentic self. When there are things you Have To or Should Do, convert them into things you Get To or Want To do by finding what feels real in them. If there any Have Tos or Shoulds that aren't imperative, delete them. You have choices!

- **When You Need to Fake It, Make It Real:** Find the good in difficult situations or personalities, which allows for more productive and positive interactions.

2. **The Law of Self-Image:** *You Have to Like You First*

   To make meaningful connections in an authentic way, you have to project the best parts of your true self. In other words, before you can expect others to like you, *you* have to like you. Many of you are aware of your basic strengths and can often exude confidence in a variety of situations, but even the most self-assured among you have moments of self-doubt. Take time to assess your value and strengthen your self-image by connecting with what you know you can contribute.

   - **You Believe What You Perceive:** Just as the ways you perceive other people become your reality about them, the ways you perceive yourself become your reality about you.

   - **Be Nice to Yourself:** This isn't just a warm fuzzy idea, it's scientifically grounded. Positive self-talk paves the way for authentic productivity and success.

   - **Change Your Tune:** Convert self-talk from negative to positive by reminding yourself regularly of your genuine accomplishments, reframing obstacles or challenges by creating clarity about your intended outcomes, and celebrating each step of the way.

   - **Fake It 'til You Make It Real:** Acting as if you have already changed your thinking or achieved a desired goal is a powerful way to grow accustomed to new thought patterns and strategies. Keep acting "as if" until you have fully absorbed them and made them real.

3. **The Law of Perception:** *Perception Is Reality—Yours and Theirs*

   Whatever impressions a person gathers of you, as they consciously or unconsciously interpret your words and actions, become their reality about you. What we perceive is what we believe to be true.

Each person has their own experiences and understands people based on their own realities. Their perception is right. The Law of Perception focuses on the realities of how others see us and the impressions you make when you first meet people. In order to understand the Law of Perception, you must also understand the sub-law of first impressions. We human beings love to be right. First impressions are critical. It is the first experience I have of you and it's how I will most likely experience you on future occasions.

- **The Sub-Law of First Impressions:** It is much easier to make a good first impression than to change a bad one. Do it right the first time.

- **We Create Our Perceptions:** Just as we create first impressions, we create the perceptions based on them. Be your authentic self to transmit that to others and impact their perceptions of you.

- **Know Your Style:** Learn your dominant communication style, and pick up on the styles of those around you to create effective perceptions and avoid misperceptions.

- **Keep an Open Mind:** Stay open to changing your perceptions of people as your connections with them grow. This also increases the likelihood that they'll stay open to changing their perception of you.

- **Be Consistent:** To positively communicate your authentic self, make sure all your modes of messaging—verbal, vocal, physical—are in sync.

- **Do Away with Self-Doubt:** Harness the strategies of Saying Nice Things, Positive Reframing, Fake It 'til You Make It Real, and Work from the Outside In to connect with your best perceptions of yourself and convey those to others.

- **Be Flexible:** Be aware of the signals you're putting out there and the ones other people are transmitting to you, and modify your behavior when necessary to ensure you're being perceived in the most authentic way.

4. **The Law of Energy:** *Energy Is Contagious*

   During any interaction, each person transmits energy that affects the dynamic of that relationship. Becoming more conscious of how you are acting and feeling, how the other person is acting and feeling, and what that combination contributes to your encounters is a powerful tool for harnessing likability and building meaningful connections. Often we are not even aware of the energy we are giving off. Energy impacts your communication, and it can either work for you or against you.

   - **Find the Right Energy:** Channeling your authentic energy doesn't mean constantly being happy—we can be genuine and real, and forge positive connections, even when faced with difficulties and challenges.

   - **Identify Your Energy and Theirs:** Recognizing your energy in a given situation helps you understand how you are contributing to the dynamic, and what you can change to affect the most positive outcome. Recognizing the energy others give off helps you adjust your own if need be to keep things on track.

   - **Energy Knowledge Is Power:** What we know about our own energy and the energy of others builds over time, and it's a crucial part of deepening connections and increasing productivity. Energy expectations are what we expect from ourselves and others based on our energy knowledge.

   - **Harness Your Networking Energy:** Determining the situations in which you express your most positive authentic energy is the key to creating the most fruitful networking opportunities.

5. **The Law of Curiosity:** *Curiosity Creates Connections*

   Genuine curiosity can lead to more authentic, engaging conversations, which may lay the foundation for sustained relationships. Even seasoned professionals who understand and have successfully built valuable connections over the years can benefit from remembering how to stay curious. Showing your genuine interest in someone else increases your likability, and you never know what opportunities may open up. Your goal is to uncover what you might have in common.

- **Start by Being Curious:** Harness your curiosity to initiate conversations and open up avenues of dialogue.

- **Learn How to Ask Questions:** Open-ended questions create opportunities for conversation; probing questions are the follow-ups that deepen the connection the conversation creates.

- **Don't Interrogate:** Stay curious, and continue asking questions to help the conversation unfold in fruitful new directions, but remember that a discussion is a two-sided thing. Sharing yourself is part of the experience and a key part of building the connection.

- **Restrain Your Internet Tendencies:** Use the internet to prep for events and meetings and build background knowledge, but don't go overboard. Knowing too much can leave you with nothing left to know, deadening curiosity and taking away that path to true communication. Moderate yourself.

6. **The Law of Listening:** *You Have to Listen to Understand*

   Just as curiosity is all about asking focused, engaged questions to find connections, listening is all about actively hearing and absorbing what is being said. Listening is not a passive activity. It takes energy and concentration to focus on what people are saying and what they mean by it, rather than hearing what you think they mean or what you want them to mean. How you listen is just as vital to strong communication as what you say, and it has just as much impact on your likability. It is crucial to do it effectively.

   - **Listen to Understand:** If we want others to understand us, we have to understand them by truly listening to what they're communicating.

   - **Harness the Three Levels of Listening:** *Listening In*, level one, relates what you hear to you and helps establish commonalities and conversational ease. Level two, *Listening Out*, relates what you hear to the speaker and leverages the Law of Curiosity to uncover interests and perspectives. *Listening Intuitively*, level three, is a powerful tool for gaining a deeper understanding of the situation and possibly even helping the speaker put words to things they haven't yet verbally expressed.

- **How You Listen Is Key:** Get off your pedestal and listen from new perspectives to encourage communication and build meaningful connections. And don't forget, sometimes good listening is done with your eyes as well as your ears.

- **Manage Distractions:** Articulate when you need to regain your focus (just say it!), jot down thoughts so that you won't be distracted trying to remember them later, and if you're too exhausted to muster the energy to truly engage, postpone and reschedule.

- **Improve Your Listening:** Take credit for the ways you already listen well, and note the areas where you can improve. Then set up a plan to work on those things.

- **Good Listening Is a Win-Win:** Not only does listening well make people feel heard and understood, it enhances your experience of the situation and of the connection.

7. **The Law of Similarity:** *People Like People Who Are Like Them*
Realizing that we share a connection with someone else puts us at ease, whatever the parallel is. Finding those similarities and associations increases your comfort with new people and, likewise, their comfort with you. This makes the conversation easier, but also opens the door to discovering what else you have in common—more links for building connections. The commonalities we have with people are not always obvious at first, but understanding how to stay alert to them is part of the work of building connections into meaningful relationships.

When meeting new people, the Law of Similarity tells us that we should be looking for commonalities or similarities to build trust. The possible ways you may connect with someone are virtually endless, and by using the Laws of Curiosity and Listening, you can discover what you have in common with someone and where your natural connections occur.

- **The Sub-Law of Association:** People trust the sources they know best. Being associated with one of those trusted sources often means that the trust will, by association, be transferred to you.

- **Uncover Connections:** Look for common interests, backgrounds, shared experiences, and beliefs to find similarities that can help build connections.

- **Be a Mirror:** When you're comfortable in a conversation and feeling engaged, communicate that by reflecting the person with your body language. Don't force it, just follow your natural mirroring tendencies.

- **It's Not Always Obvious:** Don't get stuck on the obvious differences; you never know what similarities are there for the finding.

8. **The Law of Mood Memory:** *People Are More Apt to Remember How You Made Them Feel Than What You Said*

The way you experience a person or a situation—the feeling you get, whether negative or positive—lingers long after the actual moment of interaction has past. The impressions you're left with form the feelings you associate with that person or event. This is called *mood memory*. Creating positive mood memories of yourself for other people is an essential part of increasing your likability.

The Laws of Self-Image, Perception, and Energy intertwine to help shape mood memory. The energy with which you enter a situation dictates your word choices and body language. These things transmit your energy to other people, which in turn impacts their mood memory of you and the situation. It is a cycle, one that you can consciously affect when you have awareness.

- **It's Not What You Say, It's How You Say It:** The overall energy you impart often has more of a lasting impression on someone than the specifics of what you said.

- **Harness Your Words, Your Body, and Your Energy:** The same strategies for word choice, body language, and shifting energy can be applied to creating positive mood memory. How you perceive of and present yourself will directly impact the impression you leave.

- **Admire, Appreciate, and Ask for Advice:** Articulating what you admire about someone makes them feel understood; asking for advice makes them feel valued and shows that you can be vulnerable, which fosters trust. Both are powerful tools for creating positive mood memory.

- **Know When It's Over:** Exit the conversation at the appropriate time to ensure the most positive mood memory and the best opportunities for productively following up.

9. **The Law of Familiarity:** *People Are Comfortable with Who and What They Know*

The more someone hears from you or about you, the more they will develop feelings of trust in you, and the more their comfort with you will grow. When you regularly extend yourself, in a variety of ways and for a variety of reasons, you allow connections to continue unfolding, which increases familiarity and likability.

There is, of course, a line between keeping your name in someone's mind by building positive associations and barraging them to such an extent that they tune you out. Creating mental and physical familiarity enhances likability, and it's important to develop this whether you are in or out of sight of the other person.

- **Build Familiarity:** Stay in someone's mind through social networking applications, notes of well-wishing, personal recommendations, and sending your regards.

- **Continue the Conversation:** Leverage tech tools and social networking sites to increase your opportunities to interact.

- **Keep It Authentic:** Harness electronic media tools in ways that seem natural and true to you. Don't get in someone's face: be in their circle.

10. **The Law of Giving:** *Give First, Give Because You Can, Giving Creates Value*

One of the strongest ways to increase likability and foster a connection is to demonstrate that we understand someone else's needs and are happy to help fulfill them. By drawing on what we've learned about the other Laws of Likability, we can apply our creativity to expand the kinds of value we offer others, giving to them in ways that speak directly to what might be useful for them.

There are so many ways to provide value to another person, and everyone has something to offer. Whether it's by suggesting resources, creating opportunities for meaningful interactions, or offering feedback and support, we can employ the Law of Giving by seeking out chances to give back. By embracing opportunities to help others, you can recognize all the ways, big and small, that giving adds value to your relationships.

- **Do unto Others:** There are countless ways to give freely to others, including making introductions to other people they might benefit from knowing, extending invitations to events and activities, sharing resources, doing favors, and giving advice.

- **You Can Help:** Be proactive about determining how you can help the people in your circle. Create an action plan detailing whom you're going to help and how to set the Law of Giving in motion. Then do it.

- **What Goes Around, Comes Around:** You may not always be the explicit recipient of the Law of Giving, but when you give to others more often than not, you reap rewards in return.

- **Pay It Forward:** Repay kindnesses and generosity bestowed upon you by continuing the giving—extend yourself freely to others to sustain the positive cycle of giving.

11. **The Law of Patience:** *Give It Time, Things Happen*

Patience produces results. You never know when things will happen, but with patience they do happen. This law is needed to embrace the other laws. You must have patience with yourself and with others—patience to find similarities, build the relationship, establish trust, and create familiarity. Having patience means choosing to do something without expecting to get something back. It means doing it because you can and because you want to. Being patient means knowing and trusting that somewhere in the universe, some person or some good cause is benefiting from the way you have lived the Laws of Likability.

- **It Comes Back to You, or It Goes Somewhere Else:** You may not know what the results of your generous actions will be, or whether or not you will ever directly benefit from them. That's okay. Kindness repays kindness, even if it's not in obvious ways.

- **You'll Get Your Chance:** Be patient with yourself. You never know how or when you may be able to bring value to someone else.

- **Friendships Grow in Time:** Stay open to the possibility that a relationship may evolve over time. Have patience.

Refresh Your Memory

Likability enables connection and is often the foundation for lasting connections. You can't make anyone like you: you can enable them to see what is likable about you.

1. **The Law of Authenticity:** *The Real You Is the Best You*

2. **The Law of Self-Image:** *You Have to Like You First*

3. **The Law of Perception:** *Perception Is Reality—Yours and Theirs*

4. **The Law of Energy:** *Energy Is Contagious*

5. **The Law of Curiosity:** *Curiosity Creates Connections*

6. **The Law of Listening:** *You Have to Listen to Understand*

7. **The Law of Similarity:** *People Like People Who Are Like Them*

8. **The Law of Mood Memory:** *People Are More Apt to Remember How You Made Them Feel Than What You Said*

9. **The Law of Familiarity:** *People Are Comfortable with Who and What They Know*

10. **The Law of Giving:** *Give First, Give Because You Can, Giving Creates Value*

11. **The Law of Patience:** *Give It Time, Things Happen*

3

What Level Connector Are You?

"I think anything is possible if you have the mindset and the will and desire to do it and put the time in."

ROGER CLEMENS

I HAD a theory. When I thought about the Connectors I knew, I recognized certain characteristics about how most of them think and act. As a rule, they were often accepting, trusting, and conscientious, to name just a few traits I noticed. In order to validate (or revise) my theory, I conducted an extensive survey on the attributes that I hypothesized led to a Connector approach to relationships. The survey looked at the attributes of self-esteem, conscientiousness, extraversion, emotional intelligence, trust, locus of control, political skill, and authenticity as well as behaviors about appreciation, community, and responsiveness.

In addition to the survey, I conducted extensive interviews with different types of Connectors. What I found is that my hunch was true—Connectors do have certain behaviors, ways of doing things and ways of looking at the world, all of which add up to stronger relationships. For example, 98% of Connectors are genuine during their communication with others—they don't put up walls or feign interest in someone to impress. They're also highly emotionally intelligent—Connectors are 5.5 times more likely to know their friends' emotions from their behavior than Non-Connectors.

The next section of the book will share the seven mindsets of a Connector and how you can adopt them into your way of thinking and interacting.

1. Connectors Are Open and Accepting
2. Connectors Have Clear Vision
3. Connectors Believe in Abundance
4. Connectors Trust
5. Connectors Are Social and Curious
6. Connectors Are Conscientious
7. Connectors Have a Generous Spirit

Whether or not the mindsets are already a part of your nature, you will benefit from the advice of the powerhouse experts and Connectors who share their knowledge throughout the book.

The likelihood is that all of us have some of these mindsets as part of our approach to people already. My research with the survey revealed that the differentiation on a few of these mindsets isn't large, which suggests that it's often a subtle tweak in your behavior that can take you to the next level of Connector. First, you have to determine which level you are right now. Then you can decide what type you want to be. Perhaps you are already there and simply want to enhance the level that works for you.

A Connector Defined

A **Connector** is someone with a certain way of thinking and behaving, who acts and gets results with ease because they have a level of credibility and trust in and from their network. When they ask for something or make an introduction, it carries weight and people respond.

In his book *The Tipping Point*, Malcolm Gladwell states that the most obvious criterion is that Connectors know a lot of people.[1] He further describes a Connector as someone with an impulse to connect as a personality trait.[2] Here is where Gladwell and I differ. Though I agree some people have a natural tendency toward this way of thinking and behaving, I believe anyone can infuse these actions into their interactions and, if not born a Connector, become one.

In chapter 1, I described the mindset of a Connector as a person who is people- and relationship-focused. That is the foundation, but that definition needs to be expanded. In my survey, I presented the hypothesis that a Connector is defined by the following characteristics:

- knows a lot or a diverse set of people;
- connects other people frequently and for their benefit, not for self-interest;
- likes people and enjoys meeting new people and collects acquaintances;
- displays listening and caring by remembering information about people; and
- seeks to help others in various ways.

Whereas many characteristics in the survey had moderate variations, there was one area that revealed a dramatic difference in the thinking of a Connector. Nearly 97% of Connectors agreed with the statement "I derive personal satisfaction from creating connections or bringing people together." No other area of the survey received that overwhelming of a response. What was interesting was how much less Non-Connectors felt the same way. The survey showed Connectors are more than 60% more likely to derive satisfaction from creating connections than Non-Connectors. The result shows the self-fulfilling nature of connection. Connectors simply enjoy connecting others. One basic thing anyone can do to increase their tendency to connection is find the satisfaction in the act itself, not the result that comes from it.

The Connector Spectrum

We've probably all heard the question, "Do you know so-and-so?" How many times has someone asked you that? Too many to count, probably. It is a great question to ask to find a connection point when you're first meeting someone, because finding out who you know in common can instantly build trust, rapport, and familiarity.

When asked, "Do you know so-and-so?" how often did you say, "Yes!"? Gut check: was your answer "usually yes" or "usually no" or somewhere in between? That may be your first indication as to where you fall on the spectrum from Non-Connector to Super Connector.

There are levels of Connectors—some are natural Connectors, but not all are social butterflies. As I explained, almost everyone has some Connector tendencies. Whether or not we are naturally wired with all the Connector attributes, the likelihood is that we have a few of them. How many you access regularly influences what level of Connector you are.

The difference between the levels of Connectors is based on two spectrums:

1. the breadth and depth of your connections, and
2. your tendency to initiate or respond to others.

The level of Connector you are is not fixed, not an absolute. And being a Super Connector is not necessarily the goal for everyone. Consider the categories of the spectrum, where you are now, and where you want to be.

Super Connectors and Global Super Connectors

This is the highest-level Connector possible, but not everyone needs or wants to be a **Super Connector**. The breadth of your network crosses geographic areas, demographic differences, personal interests, professional industries, and job titles. The depth of a Super Connector's network takes you up and down the ladder. You know people in all job functions and at all levels in their careers. A **Global Super Connector** has geographic depth and breadth beyond their country's borders.

If this is your level, you have contacts that are more than acquaintances in these different areas, and their reach is varied. You fully embrace the value of relationships and the Connector mindsets, and you are actively connecting—likely on a daily basis.

A misconception about Super Connectors is that they have been in their field for a while or are at the pinnacle of their careers. Not true and by no means necessary. Jared Kleinert is a perfect example. He founded an edtech company at 15 years old. "I didn't want to get stuck in a cycle of normalcy," he explains. So he then reached out to David Hassell, founder of 15Five, who ended up mentoring and eventually hiring him, all because Jared simply emailed him and asked. He's contacted and befriended hundreds of highly successful entrepreneurs by offering to help them with what they're working on; *USA Today* named him the "Most Connected Millennial." Jared coauthored the books 2 *Billion Under 20: How Millennials Are Breaking Down Age Barriers and Changing the World* and 3 *Billion Under 30: How Millennials Continue Redefining Success, Breaking Barriers, and Changing the World*, which profiles millennials from around the globe who have collectively started companies worth billions of dollars and positively impacted millions of people through their work, platform, and advocacy. When I learned all this about him, he was only 22 years old. Jared shares what he learned from millennial outliers in chapter 12. In a way, it was easier for Jared to reach out because he didn't have family responsibilities or even rent to pay: he was able to offer free assistance and many took him up on it. Teen, graduate, or well into your middle age, there are ways to connect and keep connecting. Don't let age or circumstance hold you back.

Niche Connectors

Niche Connectors have a concentration in a specific area. It could be a geographic region, industry, or job function. The breadth and depth exist, but only within the area of their niche.

My sister, April Meyers, is a great example of a Niche Connector. She's an entrepreneur and has owned her own business for more than 25 years. April knows everyone in the real estate foreclosure market in New Jersey and everyone knows her. Whether an investor, lawyer, banker, or broker, they come to April for answers. My sister is not only a Niche Connector in her industry but also in her community. She is the mother of four kids with ages spanning a decade who themselves play multiple sports and are part of diverse clubs. It is rare that someone in her town doesn't know or hasn't at least heard of April.

What makes April a great Connector is that she makes things happen. I wrote a book with NBC after my sister ran into an old elementary-school friend who was head of its digital publishing division. She didn't just have the conversation; she followed it up. She put us in touch and told us why she was doing it. Within 14 months, we landed a sponsor, produced a book, and made a resource available to returning service members for free. From the outside, it looked like I got lucky. But I don't think it was luck: I was the beneficiary of a Connector.

Giana, a woman in my community, is another perfect example. She is the hardest-working unpaid person I know and extremely connected within the area. She's on several local boards, the class parent almost every year, and the president of the PTA for two different schools! She just canceled our lunch plans because of a deadline for one of her many volunteer positions. In this community, Giana knows the what, why, and how. She's an information source and often jokingly referred to as "the mayor." Her network is this community. She doesn't have broad reach across industries or geographies, but here she is connected.

Emerging, Responsive, and Acting Connectors

Most of the world likely lives in this category. As an **Emerging Connector,** you are on the connection path. You may embody some of the behaviors but don't yet embody all the elements and mindset. Or you may embrace all the mindsets but are not consistently applying them. A **Responsive Connector** is when you are starting to initiate the behaviors, but tend to be more responsive to requests, rather than creating value opportunities. An **Acting Connector** is consistently applying and initiating more often, but has yet to develop the breadth and depth of their network. That may be enough for you and you do not need to advance beyond to be a Niche or Super Connector.

Responsive, Emerging, and Acting Connectors understand that connecting is valuable, but it doesn't necessarily come naturally. If this is you, fantastic! You are already infusing the mindsets and some of the behaviors into your activities. Remember, this is the largest category and it is a spectrum. My husband, Michael, is a great example of how you can move and advance through this category.

When I first met Michael, a natural introvert, I would have put him at the beginning of this category as an Emerging Connector. I remember when he started business school and relied on my extroverted nature to help him break into conversations. I had graduated from the same school years earlier, but I took a back seat to let him take the lead. He understood the value of relationships and his ability to initiate and prioritize them emerged.

After business school, Michael held the same job for seven years—a job he had heard about from a connection I went to business school with who referred him for the position. When he was ready to move on, he realized he needed to grow his small, but solid network. He was getting out there and people were making introductions for him; it was going well. When I encouragingly inquired, "What have you done for your network?" He responded, "Nothing yet, but I'd do anything I could if I was asked." That is a common mindset of a Responsive Connector. They are open and willing, but don't always recognize how and when they can add value and therefore don't initiate it.

During that time and through his next position, Michael joined an industry organization for people in high-level technology positions. Eventually he took a board position in the organization. He became known among his peers and often proactively shared job postings he had heard about with the members in the transition group. It became part of his thinking to consider how he could help those in his network with introductions and information. He evolved into an Acting Connector. When he was looking for that next role, he had multiple people clamoring with ideas and leads. He landed his most recent position very shortly after he began his search. When he started connecting and helping others, it made all the difference.

Non-Connectors

The last type of Connector is a **Non-Connector**—someone who doesn't see the value in it or is really uncomfortable with the idea. Those types can benefit from all of this as well—connecting doesn't have to be big, ugly, or scary. I've said it before and I'll say it again: *anyone can be a Connector.*

If you are putting yourself in the Non-Connector category, I have a few questions for you.

- *Are you being too hard on yourself?* Often we don't give ourselves credit for the things that we do. Would other people put you in this category? All of us connect, though we don't always associate the relationships we have with "being connected."
- *Do you see the value in connecting?* Perhaps this is your norm because you haven't seen the value in a different approach. Perhaps you are a bit gun-shy—a past relationship didn't work out or you didn't receive the response you'd hoped for. With a new approach and a new connection, you may get a different reaction.
- *What is one place where (or type of person with whom) you feel comfortable connecting?* You are likely already connecting but don't recognize it as such; it is just what you do. Whether it is social or professional, start where you are already. Acknowledge what works for you and build from there.

SO WHAT level Connector are you, what level do you want to be, and how do you move up? There are Connectors in every age group and region, from every background, and of all dispositions. Some have had multiple careers or been a part of multiple communities that broadened their reach. Religious organizations, volunteer groups, camps, schools, and hobbies are all places connections naturally form and develop.

You can be a Connector. Confidence and trust in yourself will bolster your ability and willingness. And—this goes without saying, but I'll say it anyway—you have to be open to different experiences and to broadening your network. Your goal shouldn't necessarily be to become a Super Connector—determine which level *you* aspire to. For example, my sister is exactly where she needs to be as a Niche Connector. If you're a Non-Connector, go for Emerging. If you're Responsive, work toward Acting. If you want to go global and become a Super Connector, do it! Honestly, if this book helps you become more of a Connector than you already are, it will be a success.

Ultimately, being a Connector is a mindset. It's not doing something: it's *being* someone. The next section of the book will examine the seven mindsets of a Connector and how you can infuse these ways of thinking and acting into your approach to people and relationships.

Refresh
Your Memory

Global Super Connectors: These Super Connectors have a broad network with geographic depth beyond their country's borders. Not everyone should strive to be this highest level of Connector.

Super Connectors: The breadth of your network crosses geographic areas, demographic differences, personal interests, professional industry, job functions, titles, and levels.

Niche Connectors: Niche Connectors have a concentration in a specific area. It could be a geographic region, industry, or job function. The breadth and depth exist, but only within the area of their niche.

Acting Connectors: Connecting has become part of your thinking. You consider how to help those in your network with introductions and information. Your network's breadth and depth are growing.

Responsive Connectors: This level is open and willing, but does not always recognize how and when you can add value and therefore you don't initiate the connection or offer of assistance.

Emerging Connectors: This is the start of connecting. An Emerging Connector embodies some of the behaviors, but not yet all of the elements and mindsets. Or you are not yet consistently applying them.

Non-Connectors: A Non-Connector doesn't see the value in or is really uncomfortable with the idea of connecting.

II

How a Connector Think and Acts: The 7 Mindsets of a Connector

Connectors have a way about them. They think and act in a way that promotes further connection and strengthens existing relationships. In my research, I uncovered the seven mindsets of a Connector. This section reveals not only the thinking of a Connector but also how anyone can adopt these mindsets and the corresponding attributes and behaviors that support connection.

4

Connectors Are Open and Accepting

"Self-love has very little to do with how you feel about your outer self. It's about accepting all of yourself."

TYRA BANKS

Real Is the Start of Relationships

There are countless reasons a Connector is effective, and yet when I sat down to write this book, I kept coming back to the fact that they are open and accepting as the qualities to lead off with. Connectors are, in a word, genuine. When they're connecting, they're not thinking about what they are going to gain or how they can leverage the relationship to their own advantage. **Authenticity is the core of likability, and openness is the foundation for connection.**

In my mind, open is the opposite of guarded. Connectors bring sincerity and even vulnerability instead of putting on a show or putting up figurative walls. You know what I am talking about—that friend who is constantly performing when they are around others. They can be entertaining, but do you feel you know who they really are? Or the colleague who is so closed off you know nothing about them outside of the office. Do you think it is possible to get to know them better? Do you even want to?

It's the same in business. I often advise people not to connect with purpose. Connect because you enjoy the relationship and understand things will come from it. There's a great maxim repeated to children all over the world: be yourself, everyone else is taken. Connectors are always willing to be themselves; they are not wearing a mask. To be open and accepting means you recognize and accept the good and "bad" aspects about yourself and, just as importantly, you accept the good and "bad" sides of others.

Awareness Is Key

The truth is, it is often easier to be accepting of others than of ourselves. You catch yourself being critical of others but will allow your inner and sometimes outer voice to be self-deprecating. To shift to a Connector mindset, you want to be aware of your strengths, weaknesses, and what I call your "unique charms." **Unique charms** is a phrase I use to describe the qualities about myself that I don't necessarily always love and that sometimes even work against me, but that I don't want to change about myself. I can flex those attributes if I am aware of them. **Flexing is the temporary, sometimes momentary, adjustment of your behavior to increase interpersonal effectiveness in an interaction.** Instead of calling a trait I possess a flaw or weakness, I consider it a unique charm and that instantly helps make the characteristic more acceptable and enables me to be more accepting of myself.

For example, one of my unique charms is my highly talkative nature. Saying I'm gregarious is an understatement. I talk more when I'm nervous; silence always used to make me uncomfortable and I would rush to fill it. For the longest time, talking was my way of trying. I have been told that sometimes it is too much and it likely has impacted my ability to connect with people. I realize I am never going to be the quiet girl and I am not trying to be. I accept this about myself. That said, by being more aware I can moderate this part of myself when it is getting in the way. I learned silence is okay and it is not my sole responsibility to keep a conversation going. I work on the habit of being the second to speak and to start by listening. I know I will get a turn to let my voice be heard and I can wait. In understanding, accepting, and flexing my own tendencies, I enable better connections to form.

It all starts with self-awareness, which is the foundation of emotional intelligence (EI). **EI is defined as the ability to recognize, express, and positively manage emotions in oneself, in others, and in groups.** The survey showed that EI, authenticity, and self-esteem play a large role in the open and accepting part of the Connector mind. Connectors are 2.6 times more likely to have high emotional intelligence than Non-Connectors, and 5.5 times more likely to know their friends' emotions from their behavior than Non-Connectors.

To develop your EI, there is self-mastery and social mastery. **Self-mastery** builds from self-awareness to self-regulation and motivation, which is your ability to respond well when your emotions are triggered, make good decisions, and overcome challenges. **Social mastery** includes empathy and social skill. See Table 4.1 for a full description.

In the survey, those who classified themselves as Connectors had higher tendencies for self-esteem and, to a lesser degree, authenticity. Connectors are 2.3 times more likely to have positive self-esteem and nearly 4 times more likely to respect themselves; they rated themselves 1.5 times more authentic than Non-Connectors considered themselves. Not surprisingly, authenticity varied by their Connector level. While more than 80% of Niche Connectors are authentic, 85% of Super Connectors are authentic—not a huge jump, but a notable one. And less than 7% of Connectors identify as feeling alienated from themselves.

Table 4.1: The Five Levels of Emotional Intelligence

SELF-MASTERY	1. Self-Awareness	You recognize and understand your own moods, motivations, and triggers and your impact on others. **Indicators:** Self-confident, able to laugh at oneself, aware of flaws and others' perceptions of self.
	2. Self-Regulation	You are able to control your reactions and think before you act or speak. **Indicators:** Conscientious, adaptable, responsive (vs. reactive), emotionally mature.
	3. Self-Motivation	You are resilient and persevere even when things don't go well. You are internally motivated. **Indicators:** Initiative, commitment, perseverance, optimism, drive.
SOCIAL MASTERY	4. Empathy	You are in tune with people's emotions. You understand their reactions and can read their nonverbal cues. **Indicators:** Perceptive, sensitive, intuitive, observant, show interest in others' needs.
	5. Social Skill	You build rapport and find common ground. You build relationships and networks. You are influential with group decision-making. **Indicators:** Strong communication and listening skills, persuasive, manage conflicts and diffuse volatile situations, inspirational.

The good news is, all of these qualities can be improved upon; they are not innate. American Express reported that employees who had undergone emotional intelligence training increased their sales 20% over those who hadn't.[1] You can improve self-awareness by asking for feedback (and being open to it from literally anyone), becoming aware of your triggers, recognizing your stress levels, and taking time to reflect. To build your social mastery, pay attention to nonverbal communication and hone your listening skills. Authenticity and higher self-esteem are every bit as trainable and worth attempting to increase even if they are qualities you already possess.

Stay Open

We all have our blind spots—an inability to make judgments about a particular issue or person, even though we may generally have sound judgment. Though it can be difficult to acknowledge our blind spots about others, it is even harder to realize them about ourselves. Part of staying open is to be aware of our own blind spots and be willing to reduce them. This is best modeled by the Johari Window developed by psychologists Joseph Luft and Harrington Ingham in 1955 to help people better understand their relationship with themselves and others. The "window" has four quadrants as shown in Figure 4.2,[2] which categorizes knowledge based on what is known by ourselves and known by others.

Figure 4.2: The Johari Window

	KNOWN BY SELF	UNKNOWN BY SELF
KNOWN BY OTHERS	I OPEN	II BLIND
UNKNOWN BY OTHERS	III HIDDEN	IV UNKNOWN

The goal is to enlarge your open quadrant (quadrant I), those things that are known by you and by others. It requires self-disclosure, shared discovery, and vulnerability to increase your openness.

Quadrant II represents your blind spot and includes information others know about you that you don't realize about yourself. To lessen your blind spot, start by seeking feedback. Asking for feedback is not the same as taking it in. I define feedback simply as information—and not all information is valuable. You do need to consider your sources and the consistency of the feedback you receive. View feedback as a gift. It is not always easy to hear, but often the information is invaluable. A few tips for receiving feedback:

- **Absorb what you are hearing.** Take it in and listen without explaining or defending, and watch your body language.

- **Ask questions.** Probe deeper into what is said; ask for examples so you can truly understand.

- **Acknowledge and agree.** Summarize what you heard and select something specific to agree with. There is usually something you will agree with.

- **Appreciate and invite.** Say thank-you—they took a risk to provide you with information. Appreciate their candor and invite them to continue to provide feedback.

- **Apply.** Put the feedback to use and, if appropriate, let them know how you implemented their feedback.

The third quadrant is known to yourself but not known to others. This is what you keep hidden from others. Perhaps these are areas of insecurity or you are being cautious with those you don't yet trust. These are the things you are not open about or not accepting about yourself, and you are likely putting on a facade and not showing up authentically. Self-disclosure and building trust will assist in shrinking this quadrant. In the last quadrant are things that aren't known to you or to anyone else around you—this is the unknown. I think of this as the "I don't know what I don't know" quadrant. It is important to remember no matter how much we do know, there is always more to learn and share. I find this quadrant motivating and humbling at the same time. Reflection, self- and shared discovery will lessen this quadrant.

The framework of the Johari Window can be intimidating. I recall a time when I thought being closed-off was advantageous. I claimed it kept me safe and comfortable. I truly thought it worked for me until someone I respected told me it didn't. I listened, but it took time. It's up to you to stay open: open to people, open to possibilities.

Accept Yourself

Accept yourself?! Hopefully your first thought is, "I already do!" Great, that is the goal. But perhaps you had a second thought and there is a part of you asking, "How the hell do I do that?" Or even "What does that mean?" Personally, both thoughts jump to my mind. I have come a long way from the doubt, self-deprecation, and self-criticism of my challenged childhood. Now I accept my unique charms as part of what makes me, me. However, that doesn't stop my brain from being hard on myself nor does it completely silence my inner judge and jury.

Part of accepting yourself is forgiving yourself. We all mess up; we're human. If you know you are having a bad day, feeling stressed out, it's perfectly okay to keep to yourself. Avoidance can be a good thing if it's for the right reasons, and giving yourself a break is allowed. Another option is to see and acknowledge the humor in the situation—you can make a joke and make fun of the state you're in, because it increases awareness for others and forgiveness.

It works great in personal as well as professional settings. Everyone gets a little cranky some days. For me, a lack of sleep puts me in a mood. For my husband, it is lack of food. I think hangry should be his middle name. Whoever "calls it" gets to be cranky without making the other person angry. Over the weekend, I turned to my husband and said, "I'm angry at you and I have no good reason to be," and then laughed. He laughed back, because he knows it's not personal. This is part of self-awareness—you *know* when you're not in a good place, and acknowledging it to those around you can help. Letting them know you're aware of your own mood ups their chances of accepting it and not taking it personally. **Shared awareness increases shared acceptance.** When you're open, you're more accepting and accepted.

And if you've done something you regret, don't sweat it. Apologize. Everyone has their moments. For example, I asked my 10-year-old son to vacuum up some foam ball pieces one of our dogs had shredded all over the floor. He's very curious how things work and decided to open up the Dustbuster, sending dirt all over our cream-colored carpet. My first reaction was annoyance and frustration. He got upset, because I don't raise my voice a lot, or I try not to. I fixed the vacuum, he vacuumed up the mess, and I apologized for overreacting. I reminded us both, "It's just dirt!" He said he overreacted too, and it was all over. It's worth remembering that in those moments when we can't control ourselves and things get away from us, we can still recover.

Acknowledgment, accountability, ownership, and recovery are all elements of acceptance. You can say you realize that what you said or did wasn't cool. It doesn't erase the fact that you did it, but you can acknowledge that what you did was wrong and that you'll try harder next time. If it's become a pattern, it helps to have a plan to change your actions so that those don't become empty promises. For example, if I'm needlessly upset about something, I try to shift my energy and find the good in the situation. You can go to the happy or calming place in your head to calm yourself. Sometimes writing your thoughts down can help release the anger or frustration. Another option is a good old-fashioned scream in your car or house where no one can hear you. It can feel great and healthy to release those feelings when nobody's around!

Not all of these tactics work in every situation, or for every person. You need to choose what is effective for the situation you're in, and give these ideas and concepts an honest effort and attempt. The first three times you try anything, it's uncomfortable and awkward and you don't want to do it. It will take you trying something five to six times before you can really judge it, and by then you'll be able to get a good sense of whether or not this can be one of your tools.

MINDSET MISSION
Increase Awareness and Act on It

Lindsay Johnson, the Radical Connector (TheRadicalConnector.com), says, "Self-acceptance isn't about hiding parts of yourself; it is about understanding it and working with it." I love her saying, "The most important connection you will make is the connection to yourself." That's why I reached out to her as an expert in self-acceptance. She agrees that you can't and don't necessarily want to change who you are. But she promotes the need to understand it, work with it, and sometimes adapt it—so that you can grow.

Lindsay divulged her reason for being is "moving people from a place of comparison, competition, and self-judgment toward fully understanding and loving themselves." Lindsay was the epitome of open when she shared her story and perspective with me. That is where she has gotten in her life, but that wasn't always the case.

"I was raised in a household where being myself was not only discouraged and punished, it often had violent and destructive consequences," she shares. "I learned at an early age that being myself was not safe."

Lindsay highlights that the world around us doesn't make it easy to feel accepted when media, advertising, and even fairy tales often bombard us with messages of shame, exclusion, and mockery. The world seems to tell people that who we are is not okay, so "buy this product!" or "try this solution!"

The result, Lindsay explains, is that countless people don't feel safe in who they are. When you don't feel safe, you play small and become invisible, or you hide who you are in order to fit in. Finding self-acceptance doesn't happen in an instant, she says—it is a journey of uncovering your true self under the layers of masks you may have worn over the years.

Self-acceptance takes time and practice. Be gentle and patient with yourself. Give yourself permission to look at yourself differently, creatively, and, as Lindsay calls it, with radical self-acceptance. To get started, I adapted an exercise Lindsay shared with me that she uses with clients to "begin to peel away the masks of who you thought you had to be and connect with who you really are." This exercise is intended to increase your awareness and enable action.

Step 1: Stop Apologizing and Self-Criticizing. Easier said than done? For a week, try writing down every time you apologize when you haven't done anything wrong. When you are mentally beating yourself up for something you did or did not do or say. You may also want to keep track of when you don't ask for what you want or need. This will increase your awareness of the situations and frequency. Awareness is the first step in initiating a shift.

Step 2: Connect with Your Confidence. To shift your thinking, note each moment in your day that you felt confident or proud. What were you doing? How did others respond to you? What about the environment or people enabled that feeling? Take notice of the positive impact you have on those around you. Create a mental picture that you can reference in times when your confidence wanes.

Step 3: Take Action. Once you recognize situations when you feel your best self, consider how you can create opportunities to access your confidence. Whether by the type of task, the people you interact with, or the opportunities you get involved in. Stretch yourself outside your comfort zone to continue to expand and grow your confidence—which enables self-acceptance. Give yourself permission to do or ask for something you have been wanting. Instead of talking yourself out of it, talk yourself into it. Visualize yourself doing it and your ideal outcome, then go for it!

Be Accepting of Others

Once you're more accepting of yourself, it is easier to be accepting of others. When you admit that you're flawed, it becomes easier to handle flaws in others. But that doesn't mean it's easy. We're all quick to jump to conclusions and judge. That's not a bad thing—it's our gut instinct, and that's okay. We are not seeking to be judgmental. Most of the time, we are just being efficient. But to be truly open and accepting, we need to be aware of the possibility that we may be wrong.

Slow Your Thinking Down

I encourage people to stay in a place of curiosity rather than conclusion. It is difficult to slow down your fast-thinking mind enough to stay curious. I use four questions to help keep an open mind. You do not have to ask yourself all four questions every time; any one of them will get you closer to curiosity and keep you open to evolve your conclusions.

The concept of slowing down your thinking is partially about giving your brain time to draw a more educated assessment of the situation, rather than a quick and potentially incorrect judgment. When you are in a situation where the interpretation of events and behaviors can have an impact on relationships, collaboration, or results of any kinds, consider testing that evaluation with these four questions:

1. What don't I know?
2. How else could I interpret it?
3. What if I am wrong?
4. Do I want to be right?

Know You Don't Know It All

Question 1. What don't I know? About this situation, person, what they've done or why they have done it? You don't know what you don't know, and sometimes you need to remind yourself that you may not have all the information. I read a fascinating article in the

Harvard Business Review about gaps in our knowledge: when asked, most people find they can't explain the workings of everyday things they think they understand.[3] I put myself to the test and you can too. Find an object you use daily (a stapler, a phone, a zipper) and try to describe the particulars of how it works. You're likely to discover unexpected gaps in your knowledge. Researchers from Yale University described the phenomenon of when people feel they understand something with greater precision, coherence, and depth than they really do as the illusion of explanatory depth.[4]

I share this to remind you (and myself) that we just don't know it all. By simply asking, "What don't I know?" you stay open to taking in additional information before forming your assessment.

Check Your Assumptions at the Door

Question 2. How else can I interpret the situation? Another form of the question is, "What could be another reason for someone's actions?" For example, if your employee or coworker is late for work, rather than thinking "Slacker! Irresponsible! Disrespectful!" come up with another reason for their tardiness. Maybe the day care center didn't open on time, their car broke down, they're not a morning person, but they work super late, or aliens came from outer space and took them for a ride.

The trick with this question is not to convince yourself that the alternatives are the truth, just to slow down long enough to realize that there are alternatives to your evaluation of the situation. You don't even have to come up with realistic reasons—sometimes you just need to think of the possibilities. It slows thinking down, and that's the goal.

Be Open to Being Wrong

Question 3. What if I am wrong? That's a powerful thought when you consider the speed at which you draw conclusions. Say someone bumps into you and keeps walking. You take that experience and assess the motives or intent of the person with no additional data. You then affix meaning based on your past experiences, assumptions, and beliefs. The next time you see them, you may snub them or avoid them. The result is you act toward them as if your conclusion is fact.

The thinking process that you go through, usually without realizing it, to get from a fact or experience to a decision or action is described by organizational psychologist Chris Argyris as climbing the **Ladder of Inference**.[5] By recognizing the rungs in the ladder, you can climb back down and stay open to being wrong in your initial race to the top. You can see the steps in the thinking process in Figure 4.3.

Figure 4.3: The Ladder of Inference

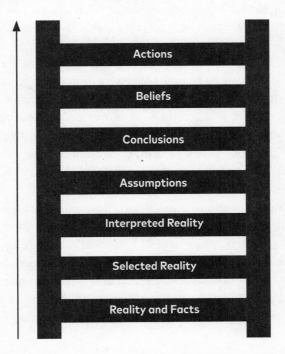

Starting at the bottom of the ladder, you observe events from the real world. From there, you:

- select facts based on your beliefs and prior experiences;
- interpret events and assign personal meaning;

- apply your existing assumptions, sometimes without considering them;
- draw conclusions based on the interpreted facts and your assumptions;
- develop beliefs based on these conclusions; and
- take actions that seem right because they are based on what you believe.

Asking yourself questions such as, "Is this the 'right' conclusion?" or "Is my judgment of the situation really based on all the facts—or on facts at all?" will continue to serve you in staying open. After all, if you're wrong in your assumptions, what's the impact on your relationship and results? Does your interpretation of the events serve you?

Don't Try to Be Right

Question 4. Do I want to be right? It can be difficult to admit, but no, you're not right about everything—the good news is, no one is. But we like to be right so we tend to seek out data that supports our foregone conclusion. We choose and interpret information to prove ourselves right. Sometimes we want to be right because "they" can't be right. We have trouble separating that person that can do no right in your world with the problem or situation at hand.

When you are working through your reasoning, pay attention to the rungs in the ladder to which you tend to jump. Do you make assumptions too easily or select only part of the data? Be aware of your tendencies so you can learn to do that stage of reasoning more carefully in the future. By using the Ladder of Inference, you can learn to get back to the facts and use your beliefs and experiences to positive effect, rather than allowing them to narrow your field of judgment.

Assume Positive Intent

At the heart of it, slowing down your thinking and recognizing when you are climbing the ladder of inference are techniques to enable you to assume positive intent. This is a challenging skill, so think of it as a tool—a tool to increase the likelihood of a more effective exchange. Assuming positive intent is at the crux of being open and accepting. It is the ability to not just be open to the idea but to believe there is a positive intention behind the words and actions of others.

Everyone has bad days, those days when we look at everything with the most negative perspective possible because we are just in that mood. I get it. Think about how that day just gets worse and worse for you. Nothing is going right, probably because you are creating that energy and outcome based on how you are approaching people and your day.

I am by no means a Pollyanna and I do not look at life through rose-colored glasses. I am aware there are many people who do not have good intentions. I do not suggest naïveté. I am by no means recommending you walk around the planet like a fool. You don't have to think everything is sunny and bright; I just want you to think it's *possible* that this situation in front of you could be sunnier and brighter than another interpretation of that same situation. I am promoting the idea that, for the most part, people are good and have good intentions.

Now you may be thinking, "What happens when a colleague has done something that clearly wasn't very positive?" For example, when a coworker suggests and attempts to take credit for an idea that *you* already suggested? Calling them out in an attack will only make you look petty. Instead, verbalize it toward a positive path. You might say, "Thank you so much for your support of my idea—I'm really glad we're aligned on this one." You're not saying, "Hey, you stole my idea!" You are positioning it as a positive—that they're championing you. By acting as if they had positive intent, you cause them to step up to that interpretation.

As I explain in chapter 4 of *The 11 Laws of Likability*, energy is contagious, and so is positivity. When you bring openness and positive assumptions to your interactions with others, they will have a positive mood memory of you. We all know positive intention isn't always the case, but trust me: in general, it's better to give people the benefit of the doubt. It will shift all of your interactions—you'll be kinder, more understanding, and more willing to listen. You won't put others in the uncomfortable position of defensiveness. I believe people can rise or fall to your expectations. By assuming the good, you provide someone the invitation to rise to that expectation. As a result, you will find you have a greater ability to connect with others. When you are accepting of yourself and accepting of others, you open up the potential for deeper relationships.

Refresh
Your Memory

Authenticity is the core of likability; **openness** is the foundation for connection.

Awareness is key to self-acceptance. To shift to a Connector mindset, you want to be aware of your strengths, weaknesses, and unique charms.

Unique charms are qualities about yourself that you don't always love and which sometimes even work against you, but you don't want to change them.

Flexing is the temporary, sometimes momentary, adjustment of your behavior to increase interpersonal effectiveness in an interaction.

The Johari Window is a model to help people better understand their relationship with themselves and others, which highlights our blind spots. To expand your open quadrant requires self-disclosure, shared discovery, and vulnerability.

The five levels of emotional intelligence cover self-mastery (self-awareness, self-regulation, and self-motivation)—which is your ability to respond well when your emotions are triggered, make good decisions, and overcome challenges—and social mastery, which includes empathy and social skill.

The Ladder of Inference is the thinking process you go through, usually without realizing it, to get from a fact or experience to a decision or action often with untested assumptions.

Slow your thinking down to be more accepting of others. Use these four questions to stay in a place of curiosity rather than conclusion:

1. What don't I know?
2. How else could I interpret it?
3. What if I am wrong?
4. Do I want to be right?

5

Connectors Have Clear Vision

"If you don't know where you are going, any road will get you there."

LEWIS CARROLL

You Have to Know Where You Are Going to Get There

Clear vision goes along with an open and accepting mindset but takes it further. There are two components to clear vision. First, you have clarity on who you are and how you can be useful—you have high self-esteem. As a Connector, you will have a strong sense of your own strengths, who is in your network, and how you can be valuable to those around you. In a nutshell, you have knowledge and confidence around the value you bring. If this is a challenge, take a look at chapter 2 in *The 11 Laws of Likability* and try the ideas there. Another option is to download the three words branding exercise from my website at MichelleTillisLederman.com: spend the time to identify your strengths and define your brand.

The second component to clear vision, and perhaps more impactful on your results: you have to know your goals. You are clear on what are you working on, where you want to go, and how you plan to get there. That classic interview question, "Where do you see yourself in 1, 5, and 10 years?" A Connector with clear vision can often answer without hesitation because they have already thought about it and are likely working on it.

If you think of yourself as a Connector and the thought of where you will be in 10 years is a foreign concept, don't fret. I don't know either! Vision does not have to be about a long-term plan; it could be about the next step. The idea is that you know what you are working on right now, why you are working on it, and where you want it to lead—even if that is only a six-month target.

To get wherever you dream of going, you have to know exactly where you're headed. Rare is the traveler who sets out without a map or, these days, a GPS! Connectors know that when they define their vision—say, they want X type of client or X type of skill—they give it power. They create a road map for their goal just by naming it. Self-esteem supports your vision. You believe in yourself, your future accomplishments, and your ability to get there. But first you have to define your goals.

The survey showed Connectors are nearly 1.6 times more likely to feel like they have control over aspects of their life than Non-Connectors. Ask yourself how much you agree with these statements:

- "When I make plans, I am almost certain to make them work."
- "I can pretty much determine what will happen in my life."
- "When I get what I want, it's usually because I worked hard for it."
- "My life is determined by my own actions."
- "Whether or not I get to be a leader depends mostly on my ability."

More than 80% of the time, Connectors agreed with these statements indicating they feel they get what they want because of their actions. A large part of feeling in control—whether you're driving a car or driving your career—is knowing exactly where you're going.

Get Clear

Every year, I write my goals on a Post-it. Yes, my oh-so-formal goals are captured on a three-square-inch piece of paper. That is all I need to contain my entire vision for the next 12 months—or what's important, anyway. If it doesn't fit on that sticky note, it doesn't count as a goal for me. And, theoretically, it doesn't get my attention. Everyone sets goals in different ways, and there's no right or wrong way to do it, but keeping it simple helps.

You might consider using a SMARTER goal model for each dream on your career or personal bucket list. There are many variations to the model, though they usually cover these main aspects.

Specific. This is the number-one criterion for making a clear goal. You have to be exact about what you are trying to accomplish. The more specific and broken-down the goal, the higher the probability of achieving it.

Measurable. When setting goals, ask yourself, "How will I know that I did it?" That is your measurement. It is your indicator of progress. Your measurement can be time (do it this fast or by this time), quantity (finish this many or lose this much), frequency (do it this often), quality (do it with this level of accuracy or less than this number of errors, complaints, or returns).

Actionable. Is it something you can do something about? Is there action to be taken to move the goal forward? If so, it is actionable. To be actionable does not mean the action needs to be taken by you. It could be assignable to someone else as a means toward your goal. For example, one of my personal goals is to no longer do the dishes. Therefore, I have to either eliminate the task or assign it to someone else to act on it.

Realistic. Realistic can be tricky. You want a goal to be challenging but achievable. Consider the resources, competing priorities, your knowledge, and time when setting the goal. Stretch yourself, but make it attainable. If it is unrealistic, it can become demotivating.

Timed. Without this aspect, it is just a thought, not a goal. Give yourself a deadline. By when or how long after will you accomplish it? Setting several time-bound steps along the way can help keep you on track.

Most SMART models end here. I advocate a SMARTER model to include two additional factors that are critical to your vision.

Engaging. If the goal is not engaging or meaningful to you, it is hard to be motivated to act on it. This is the "why" behind the "what" of the goal. Ask yourself, "Why is this goal important?" and "Why is it important to me?" Is it something you truly *want* to do or is it something you feel you *should* do?

Revisited. This is key. Evaluate your progress, set milestones, and revisit the appropriateness of your goal. If the goal is no longer relevant, realistic, or engaging, why are you doing it? It is okay to reset your goals and move up or back a timeframe with additional information or resources at your disposal. Adjusting your goal is better than abandoning it, if it is still one that makes sense for you.

I personally believe it's wise to keep goals doable within the next year. It's when people set goals for 10, 15 years down the road that they struggle. Thinking so far into the future may not help us in the present. You might want kids *and* a corner office on Wall Street by a certain age, but what are you doing in the next six months to make it happen? Having clear vision is a necessary step to help get you there.

MINDSET MISSION
Take Action toward a Goal

There are things we think about but don't actually work toward. I am fond of the saying, "A goal without a deadline is just a dream."

I had been thinking about writing this book for a while. The idea seemed too big to tackle. I created a laundry list of things I needed to do to get the book done—then picked one. I thought about one thing I could do to work toward it and developed the survey. Then I promoted the survey, then analyzed it, and eventually...

What do you want to accomplish? Take five minutes, and put it on paper. Think of a goal you have, and apply the SMARTER model to refine it. Once you are clear on the goal, the next question to ask yourself is, "What is one small thing I can do to make progress?" Answer these three questions to get yourself started:

1. What is one thing I can do to make progress toward my goal?
2. Who is one person who could help me?
3. When will I take this step?

Now that you put a plan in place, it is time to execute it. When the whole plan is daunting, defining one to-do and checking it off your list feels great. When it's done, ask the question again. Make it weekly— say, "Every Friday, I'm going to ask, 'What's one thing I can do within the next seven days to make progress?'" Get an accountability buddy and set a call once a week to discuss what you've done to get closer to each of your goals. Movement begets momentum, so simply start something.

Keep Talking

A clear vision is not just knowing where you want to go but understanding what it will take to get there. There are things a Connector does to move from vision to accomplishment. They will talk about what they're working on with comfort and ease; they are comfortable asking for help and actually accepting help, which is often harder. Connectors are clear about what would be helpful to them to achieve the goal they are working on.

When I was still in my finance job, I had a goal to start my own business. I did volunteer work for an animal-rescue organization called Stray from the Heart. Every year, we put on the Canine Comedy benefit. A gala event with celebrities, puppies, and lots of volunteers to help. I chaired the event along with my friend, Donna, who was working for JP Morgan at the time. Through our weeks of planning, I had been telling her that I wanted to start my own training and coaching company and how I was working toward it.

The day of the event we had more than 200 volunteers; I didn't know the name of the guy who approached me and said he worked with Donna as a temp employee and Donna had told him what I was working on. I smiled distractedly as there was so much to do but couldn't help myself from jumping on the invitation to share. Within minutes, he asked, "Do you want to meet my boss?"

"Who is your boss?" I asked.

"The head of JP Morgan's investment banking training department."

I picked my jaw up off the floor, nodded vigorously at a momentary loss for words, and then simply said, "Yes please, thank you!"

That meeting landed me JP Morgan as my first client in my yet-to-be-formed new company, Executive Essentials. I didn't have business cards yet, I hadn't filed the LLC paperwork, and I had no website, but I had my first client. My dream was happening because I was clear on it and kept talking about it. Although I can't remember that guy's name, I do remember him telling me my energy and passion for what I was working toward was palpable. He said that is what made him make the offer of an introduction.

I have heard pushback on this piece of advice in the past. Either because you don't want your current company finding out or from fear that someone will steal your idea. Those are perfectly valid concerns, and worth considering. To protect yourself from someone stealing your idea, there are things you can do—both formal and informal—when you're talking to people. You could have someone sign an NDA or you could file for patent or trademark for a bit of legal protection. You can refrain from talking in specifics. For example, you could tell them you're looking for someone to design a wireframe for your app, and you don't have to reveal what the app idea is. If you don't want people at work to know what you're secretly working on, no problem. Be selective—only tell the people you truly trust, and let them know it's confidential. Alternatively, only share it with people outside your industry for a bit of separation.

When I was transitioning from my finance career into this one, I knew I was on the right track because I couldn't stop talking about it. What I was working on was exciting and interesting to me, and the more someone asked about it, the more enthusiastic I became in my response. If you don't want to talk about what you are doing (excepting those times when an NDA or current company position prevents it), maybe you aren't doing the thing you really want to do. People feel your enthusiasm and they'll want to jump on board. But if you are not feeling it, they won't be either. So talk, and keep talking.

Accept Help

People don't always feel comfortable accepting help, much less asking for it. Some Connectors can have a hard time with it too. I know I do. I'm really good at giving help and dispensing my hard-learned experiences and expertise, but I struggle with accepting help, even when it's offered. If you are thinking that sounds like you, ever wonder why?

Giving help makes you feel strong, useful, and purposeful. It is easy to feel good about yourself when you give. Accepting help often has the opposite effect, evoking feelings of weakness. Sometimes you feel like a pain in the assets (recovering CPA humor). You worry about annoying your contacts or being too pushy. I have felt all of that and, as a result, I don't always ask as much as I could or need to.

But here's the thing we all need to recognize: if *we* feel good about giving help, others do too. It helps to remind yourself that when you are asking for help, you are affording the other person the opportunity to feel useful and purposeful. When you are infusing the Connector behaviors into your interactions, people will want to add value to you and your goals, just as you're doing for them. Reciprocity is not a bad thing; it is one of the ways that the impact of Connectors gets amplified. Reciprocity triggers a desire not to owe if you have been the beneficiary. I prefer to think of it as inspiring the desire to give. Either way, people who receive will just feel better if they can give too.

Occasionally, you might not actually need the help being offered. You don't have to accept help you don't need. But my advice is to not dismiss it. Don't say, "No, no, don't worry about me, I'm okay." Dismissing an offer of help like that doesn't make anyone feel good. It's perfectly okay to acknowledge and appreciate their attempt, and let them know that if needed, you'll come back to them. Then actually come back to them!

How to Find Your Balance with Work, Life, and Connecting

Mary LoVerde (MaryLoVerde.com), is a work–life balance expert and change catalyst, a job title that didn't exist in the recent past. But in today's harried times and changing workplace, it has become a vital role. We may not all have one of these in our company or life, so you may need to fill those shoes yourself. In chapter 6, there are tips on how to make time for connecting. Here, Mary provides advice on how to think about work–life balance more broadly. Mary explains, "We have irrefutable scientific proof that we thrive when we feel connected to what matters most to us. So instead of constantly asking, 'What do I need to do?' ask a better question, 'With whom or what should I connect?' This is what will make us feel good—and feeling good is what life balance is all about." Here are three more ideas from Mary:

1. **Use Rituals.** Mary recommends creating a daily ritual to help ground you. A ritual can be meditating for 10 minutes every morning, filling in your gratitude journal, or exercising daily. You can also have rituals or habits around nurturing your network such as setting up a lunch twice a month or reaching out to three contacts a week. As Mary explains, "A meaningful ritual allows you to build in some predictability and stability into your busy schedule."

2. **Take Breaks.** It hits home for me when Mary states, "When you add and add without stopping in math it is called infinity. When you add and add without stopping in life, it is called insanity." Taking a break is so important for productivity and rejuvenation that many cultures build it in—for example, afternoon tea and siestas. A break can be as simple as turning off your phone for 15 minutes, going for a walk around the block, or reading something inspirational in the middle of the day. Even better, take that walk or have that tea with a friend or colleague. When you find yourself giving into the urge to push through too often, create breaks. My break is putting a few pieces into the current jigsaw puzzle on the dining room table.

3. **Pick Sleep Over Technology.** Studies prove time and again that sleep is imperative for our mental and physical health. As Mary put it, "That last 30 minutes at night of Candy Crush, email, or LinkedIn cannot compete with the benefit of a half hour more sleep each night." Often we don't function at full capacity when we have a bad night's sleep. Given the choice between technology and sleep, prioritize rest.

Ask for What You Want

I will never forget the first time I received backlash from an audience member. It was shortly after *The 11 Laws of Likability* came out. I was giving a speech on relationship networking and passionately encouraging people to live the Law of Giving. I was stopped in my tracks when a woman in the front of the audience loudly grumbled, "I'm tired of giving. Where's mine?" Momentarily speechless, my eyes caught hers and she looked mortified that what she was thinking came out of her mouth so loudly. I am glad it did.

I engaged her and she threw her hands up in the air, clearly relieved to get it off her chest, and continued: "No one ever gives back." Trying to think on my feet as to why it may be happening I went through ideas under my breath... Was she giving to the wrong people? No, that isn't it. Was she giving the wrong things? I dismissed that too. Then I looked at her and asked, "What have you asked for?" With a look of something between surprise and confusion, she thought about it for a moment and then, a bit deflated, said, "Nothing." Aha, we found the reason!

Connectors understand that they need to ask. But asking is scary. What if they say no? What if they think I am rude or pushy, or what if they don't remember me at all? We can get in our heads and talk ourselves out of asking. Connectors with a clear vision know not only that it is *okay* to ask, but that you actually *have* to ask. As Wayne Gretzky said, "You miss 100% of the shots you don't take." If you don't ask, the answer is *no*. Asking immediately increases your odds of getting the help you need. There are ways to ask that alleviate some of the potentially negative interpretations of your request and don't put the longer-term relationship at risk. First, get clear on your fear. Are you worried about putting them on the spot, inconveniencing them, or even jeopardizing the friendship by making them feel uncomfortable? Then choose a strategy to counter your concern. Below are four pressure-free "asks" that snuff out the stress from these situations for you and the person you are asking.

Four Types of Asks

1. **The Opt-Out Ask.** A yes is easy, and a no is hard. People may want to say yes, but they may need or have to say no. Make it as easy to say no as it is to say yes. Because if they have to say no, you don't want them to be uncomfortable. If they are uncomfortable, then they'll want to avoid you; they feel bad about saying no. That could put the longer-term relationship at risk. The Opt-Out Ask gives them the reason they can use to say no right in the request. Try "If you have the time" or "If your company allows it." And to reinforce it, add "If not, no problem, I understand." This makes it okay for them to say no and leaves the door open for a yes down the road.

2. **The Make-It-Easy Ask.** Just because you give an opt-out doesn't mean you want a no. So the easier you can make the ask, the more likely you are to get it. Making it easy is all about giving the person you are asking options on how to help.

- **The Alternate Ask.** This is the either/or ask. You could help me this way or that way. The asks are typically of equal value to you but one may be preferable to them, so provide the option for them to choose.

- **The Shrinking Ask.** This is also an either/or ask, but the second ask is typically a smaller request. For example, "Can we grab lunch or maybe just a coffee?" If you are not at a yes yet, you may then offer something even smaller: "Would a call be easier or if you are too busy, is there someone else you can connect me with?" The idea is to keep making the request smaller until it is something they can say yes to.

- **The Convenient Ask.** This one should be used when the request is to someone who is bringing more to the table or is higher on the hierarchy. You make it as convenient for them as possible. "Do you want me to come to your office or do you have a favorite coffee shop?" "Is 2 p.m. better or 3 p.m.? Whatever works for you works for me." You want to defer to them as to what their preferences are in the execution of the request.

3. The Non-Ask. This ask doesn't look like a request at all and, as a result, is one of the easiest to attempt. With the Non-Ask, you are not requesting anything specific. Instead you are sharing what you are working on or a current goal. For example, rather than asking how to make my book a bestseller, I might say, "What I'm working on right now is making my book a bestseller." That triggers the other person's desire to help. It's in our nature to be helpful and useful, and just laying out your desires can prompt them for some much-needed advice. If the ask is too subtle, add, "Any ideas for me?" Everyone wants to have an idea. Then just listen.

4. The WIIFT Ask. WIIFT stands for *what's in it for them*. This ask leads with the benefits for the other person. Think about how it might help them to do the thing you are asking. Say you want to go to a conference and want the company to pay for it. You know why you want to go and what is in it for you (**WIIFM**—*what's in it for me*). That may not make the company want to shell out thousands of dollars. What does the company get out of you attending? Some forward-thinking organizations include in their invitation to conferences a section on the benefits to share with your manager. Word of warning when using the WIIFT Ask, don't pretend that there is a benefit to someone when there is not. You are better off acknowledging the difference in ability to help. In other words, don't tell the CEO of a company it will be to their benefit to talk to you if you are fresh out of college. Instead, be honest about what you will get and add, "I am not sure if I can be of value to you, but I am happy to provide my generation's perspective or discuss different online platforms if you are interested." That way you show your intent to add value and sometimes that is enough.

How Not to Ask for Help

I recently received a LinkedIn request from a complete stranger. There's nothing unusual about that; I always welcome new connections and often send a note. (See more on my tips and tricks for LinkedIn in chapter 11). But once in a while, I get one that I can use as a teachable moment. In the invitation to connect, I received the following note:

> *Hi Michelle. Please look at my profile, check out my résumé, and let me know if you know of anyone who can assist me in a profitable career. I would greatly appreciate that.*

I must admit my immediate thought was "Seriously?!" While I appreciate the boldness, there is a right way and a wrong way to ask for help, and that request was all kinds of wrong. We hadn't connected yet and already I was being told, not asked, what to do. It was off-putting to say the least. There is nothing wrong with reaching out to those who may be able to help you. Perhaps if the email said something about why they had contacted me, or that they followed my work and then asked if I would consider or be open to providing some guidance—I may have had a very different response.

If you read my first book, you might recall a story I shared in the Law of Patience chapter about Randi. Randi was the colleague who asked me for a client introduction within the first 10 minutes of meeting me. It was bold, but I admired her courage to ask. I respected it, but I was also put off by it. As a Connector, I wouldn't make a request that quickly. I'm not immediately thinking, "What can you do for me?" It felt very *me, me, me*, as opposed to the Connector mindset, which is *you and me*. I don't want to discourage you from asking in any way. If you know what doesn't work, you may feel more comfortable with the approach you choose.

What Do You Want?

I always ask people, "What do you need, what do you want, and how can I help?" If you want to formulate a clear vision, know your answers to those questions. Be clear on how you can help and the kind of help you need. The more you talk, the more people will have the opportunity to fulfill those requests. The more you listen, the more you will have the chance to help them.

Refresh
Your Memory

Clear vision means you know who you are, how you can be useful, what you are working on, and what assistance you need.

SMARTER goals is a model to evaluate and refine goals for increased clarity and actionability.

Specific. Be specific about exactly what you are trying to accomplish.

Measurable. Make it measurable so you can determine when it is done. This is your indicator of progress.

Actionable. Ensure there is something you can do about it, an action you can take toward the goal.

Realistic. A realistic goal is challenging but achievable.

Timed. Create a deadline or frequency. This creates an end.

Engaging. Determine the source of your motivation to complete the goal.

Revisited. Evaluate the progress of your goal by setting milestones and reassessing along the way.

Find balance with a daily ritual to ground you, take breaks for rejuvenation, and prioritize good sleep.

Asking is hard but necessary. Leverage different approaches to asking to alleviate resistance.

The Opt-Out Ask. Make it as easy to say no as it is to say yes. Provide a reason they can use to decline right in the request.

The Make-It-Easy Ask. The easier you can make it, the more likely you are to get it. Making it easy is all about giving the person you are asking options on *how* to help.

The Non-Ask. Don't make a specific ask; instead share your objectives and open the door for assistance.

The WIIFT Ask. WIIFT stands for *what's in it for them*. This ask leads with the benefits for the other person. Think about how it might help them to do the thing you are requesting.

6

Connectors Believe in Abundance

"People who believe they can succeed see opportunities where others see threats."

MARSHALL GOLDSMITH

Scarcity Is Scary

A Connector believes in abundance: an abundance of opportunities, an abundance of work, and an abundance of relationships. And yet fear of scarcity is ingrained in many of us. I get it. Growing up, I thought of myself as a "have not" living in a community of people who had a lot more than my family. Abundance is one of the most challenging mindsets to adopt.

My sister and I grew up in a single-parent home. Money was very tight. I remember empty rooms in our house: my mother had sold the furniture to cover the mortgage. I wore the same dress for picture day three years in a row. (It helped that I didn't grow much!) She was creative and inventive, and we always had what we needed. I learned not to ask for things because I knew we couldn't afford them. A new outfit for the first day of school just wasn't in the budget.

After college, financial security was a priority, and spending money was something I had to learn to get comfortable with. It was scary. Funny how close that word is to *scarcity*. Scarcity is scary, and scarcity thinking is based in fear. Having an abundant mindset is the opposite—it's knowing and believing that there will be enough for you and everyone else. In this chapter, we'll discuss what that truly means and how you can overcome a scarcity mindset.

First, you need to determine if you currently tend toward scarcity or abundance. If you're not sure which way you lean, take a look at Figure 6.1 for a comparison of scarce versus abundant thinking. Which column resonates for you? Our thinking is often rooted in our experiences: how we grew up, how our parents thought. Reflecting on your past can help you understand your current mindset and how it translates to your personal and professional decisions and actions.

Figure 6.1: Scarce versus Abundant Thinking

	SCARCE	ABUNDANT
PERSPECTIVE	Nothing goes right for you. You feel unlucky or like a victim. You expect the worst outcome. You worry there is not enough. You may withhold, hoard, detach, not try, or give up quickly.	You believe things will have a positive outcome. You're in charge: when things go poorly, you see how you may have impacted the outcome. You take responsibility, risks, and action.
EMOTIONS	Worried, fearful, anxious, negative, skeptical, pessimistic, and vulnerable.	Positive, confident, in control, optimistic, empowered, capable, and content.
INTERNAL MESSAGING	I can't. I shouldn't. It won't work. There isn't enough. I have to protect what's mine.	I can. I will. It will work out. There is enough to go around.
STANCE	Tentative, stuck, does not act.	Bold, confident, takes action.

Acknowledge the Fear

The first step in addressing and alleviating the feeling of scarcity is to acknowledge the fear. This was the advice I got from podcaster Jordan Harbinger (JordanHarbinger.com/Podcast). With the number-one self-help show on iTunes, Jordan is a strong believer in the abundant mindset, perhaps because he too defeated the scarce mindset.

Jordan used to be competitive and withholding. He describes the scarce mindset as spiral thinking: "You tell yourself a catastrophic story about what will happen, like, 'I don't want to make the introduction because I will have used up my goodwill,' or 'They will become better friends than we are.'" Similar stories have run through my head. For example, I had a moment of hesitation making an introduction to my editor. I had to shut out the fear that she would become too busy for me or raise her rates.

In those moments when you catch yourself making decisions from a place of fear, ask yourself *why*. What are you really afraid of? Then change the narrative in your mind. Jordan explains, "Things that are stopping you don't have to be likely or probable in any way. The possibility just has to exist in your head to hold you back." Even if the fear is reasonable, not making those introductions or not helping that person may do more harm to your psyche, relationships, and success than it does good in terms of protecting you from whatever narrative is in your head.

We all have fears, so I appreciated it when Jordan asserts that "fear is okay. There is no shame with the fear." He advises you deconstruct the shame around it. For most people, he explains, it is the realization that we act out of fear because we don't necessarily have enough trust in ourselves . . . yet!

Don't Judge Yourself in Relation to Other People

Part of trusting yourself, your skills, and your value is to stop the constant comparison against others. We judge ourselves in relation to other people and make ourselves feel better or worse as a result. Building internal confidence will help access an abundant mindset.

Jordan suggests you look to build other pillars of security. He admits, "I used to withhold things. I realized I was doing that because I was worried about other people getting ahead of me, and then what was I going to do? They're going to get an interview and they're going to do a better one, and then I'm going to lose my listeners and I'm going to be out of a job."

Jordan had to contend with the catastrophic story he had spun. To do that, he asked himself, "How else besides being miserable and hoarding all my good relationships, which I know has negative consequences, can I remedy that?" Jordan's answer was to get really good at interviewing and at producing the show. And he is! I've done hundreds of interviews, and my first time on his show he took me completely off-guard. It was a totally different interview than I had given before. I remember thinking, "I am giving the worst interview ever." It turned out to be one of my best! Jordan no longer worries about losing listeners because somebody else has the same guest. As he puts it, "Because I work on the part that I bring to the table, and not just the part the guest brings to the table, I become irreplaceable. I bring the value myself." If your only pillar of security is your relationships, you don't want to share them. Other pillars of security could be confidence in your expertise, a competency you have, or anything you find where you have a strength.

The good news is, it doesn't have to be a unique strength. I remind myself of this all the time when I can't help but compare myself to other speakers. I admire someone's exacting word choice, the tightness with which they tell a story, the structure and organization end to end. An abundant perspective enables me to realize there can be other great speakers out there and that doesn't minimize what I can do. It's really a self-comparison, not a comparison to other people. Remind yourself, "I am good at this." Whatever *this* is for you. And it doesn't matter if other people are good at it or better, all that matters is that you are good at it. Feeling a sense of competency enables what Jordan refers to as "situational confidence." True confidence doesn't depend on what other people have. Get rid of the if/then mentality: *If they are good, then I am bad* or *if they are not skilled, then my skills will shine.* He hits the nail on the head: "It's not about beating other people; it's about seeing the value *you* are creating."

Allow Others to Shine

It is natural to evaluate yourself against other people at work; after all, that is what your boss is doing when deciding who to promote. I will never tell you to minimize yourself, silence yourself, or negate your contributions. Step into the spotlight and don't be afraid to shine. As you climb higher up the metaphorical ladder, allowing others to shine reflects an abundant perspective.

Transitioning from being an individual contributor to a manager of people is a time of uncertainty. You are used to doing it all yourself and feel the sense of accomplishment in getting the job done. But the job you have now is different. You are now evaluated on what you accomplish with and through other people. You are performing well when your team performs well; it is a hard shift to make.

One of my coaching clients was in this situation and struggled with how much to take on herself. Her superiors told me she was too invested in the details and needed to learn to let others be the experts. My advice to her was to give the people on her team the chance to shine. Even if she thought she could accomplish a particular task better and faster, she had to stand back and allow her colleagues the chance. One simple way to do that is to literally take a step back in meetings—to put yourself in the back seat in the room. This positioned her team as the ones who would answer the questions, and she jumped in only when needed.

You can still have authority when you're giving the floor to someone else, and especially when you're praising them in front of your team. When you shine the light on others, it reflects back on you. As a manager, there's nothing better than a glowing, happy, and highly functioning team.

Give Credit

Giving credit is another way to allow others to shine and to remove the constant comparison between yourself and others. In one of the most comprehensive studies about job satisfaction, Boston Consulting Group surveyed more than 200,000 people around the world. They found the number-one factor for employee happiness on the job is being appreciated for their work.[1] Recognizing other people in big and small ways goes a long way to building the relationship and maintaining an abundant mindset.

The acknowledgment does not have to be for a monumental accomplishment. My son recently decided to become a vegetarian. He is already a picky eater and is sensitive to dairy. Overwhelmed by the limited options of what to feed him, I asked my sitter for advice. She researched how to cook tofu and brought in rice and beans leftover from her own dinner for him to try. I thanked her for going above and beyond to help us figure out how to honor his vegetarian preference. That simple statement garnered a huge smile and the look of satisfaction and pride stayed with her for hours.

Giving credit means just as much to entrepreneurs, who may not have an opportunity to receive as much mood-boosting praise as people who work in a busy, corporate environment. Early in my speaking tenure, I gave a speech to a local Women in Technology group. A few years later, I was asked back to keynote at their national conference. A woman who had seen both presentations came up to me afterward and said, "You have grown so much!" That positive feedback still sits with me to this day. I was speechless; I knew she didn't mean my height—she felt I'd improved! It meant so much to see that she had seen growth in me, and it fueled me to keep honing my skills.

The one thing I wish I'd asked her is *how* I grew—which brings me to my next point. When you're giving credit, be specific. Tell them what they said or did that worked and why it worked, so they can do it again and in other ways. If you want to take it a step further, let them know the impact it had on the project, the result, or you personally.

Acknowledging success is a powerful way to see opportunity and stay optimistic. Giving credit to others is often easier than giving yourself credit. There is one tactic I share with everyone who ever works for me: keep a success file. Maintain a record of testimonials or kind emails you've received. If it wasn't written, write it down yourself and document your accomplishments or the nice things someone said about you after the meeting. It can be a physical or virtual folder. Either way, it is extremely helpful at review time but also on a bad day when you need to remind yourself of the positive impact you have had.

See the Opportunity

Back in my finance days in the '90s and slightly beyond, there were very few women at the top of the organizational ladder. As a woman in a male-dominated field, it was hard not to notice and be drawn to the few who had broken through. We all wanted the one female partner in the firm to be our mentor, yet she mentored none of us.

I was surprised that the women at the top weren't reaching back to help pull other women up with them. Apparently, this was not uncommon at the time. (I am so glad times have changed!) Eventually I understood the behavior was driven by scarce thinking. The belief was, there is only room for one woman at the top. With that perspective, every other woman became a potential threat rather than an ally. I actually heard one woman say, "They are only going to make one woman a partner, and it's going to be me."

It is true that opportunities were scarce. However, just because there hadn't been multiple female partners in the past doesn't mean there can't be more in the future. Connectors don't see the status quo as the way things always have to be. They believe and act as if they can redefine it. They see the opportunity.

Though times have progressed, the scarce mentality remains. In my current field, I have had other coaches and trainers prefer not to connect, stating, "We're in competition with each other." My philosophy has always been that I don't have competitors, I have strategic partners. It can be beneficial to know people in your field, especially those with a similar skill set. For example, if I can't accept a speaking job, being connected with other people in my area of expertise means I can refer them and therefore still be valuable to the client. I also worry about the day that I can't do a scheduled talk due to a canceled flight or illness. If I can't be where I need to be, it is comforting to know there is someone who can fill in. If I viewed everyone as a competitor, I wouldn't have anyone to call to take my place.

Squash the thinking of "there are only so many ____." Whatever you fill in the blank with, that thinking is limiting. It limits your possibilities, your reach, and your results. Once you adopt the abundant mindset, it becomes a habit. You will experience reciprocity, your internal confidence grows, and you begin to see opportunity in every situation.

Realize There Is Enough

There are two ways to look at my childhood. It is much easier for me to now look back and see both perspectives—though even at the time, I could see them. My mother had instilled the importance of volunteering at a young age. I saw real need. So even when I felt like all my friends had more than me, I also always felt I never went without. I always had enough: enough food, enough clothing, and certainly more than enough love.

Scarcity is the feeling that there is never enough so you need to protect "your" piece. The objective is to shift to the belief that there is enough. It isn't easy. I remember when I transitioned from a solo practitioner to building a company where the majority of the work is done by others on my team. There were definitely moments of fear and concern. I worried I might be handing my clients to my contractors. By enabling them to build a strong relationship with the client and execute the work, they could cut me out of the equation. But I didn't give in to the fear.

It took both the abundant and trust mindsets to overcome that line of thinking. I trusted in the relationships I had built with both my clients and my contractors (more on trust in the next chapter). I also made the decision to believe that there was enough work for all of us. There was no need to steal a client. Choosing abundance became a self-fulfilling mindset. Because I enabled my team to work with my clients the way I would have, my company developed a stellar reputation. Clients trusted that I would select a great trainer for their audience and more work came. Abundant thinking is viewing the proverbial glass as half full, not half empty. A Connector maintains that belief and overcomes the moments of doubt.

Feel It, Shift It

Coming from a place of abundance doesn't mean you never have moments of envy. Everyone feels jealousy; it's a part of life. You can use the feeling: not to be competitive with someone but to be motivated by them and what they accomplished. View it as a learning opportunity, instead of wasting your energy in a way that doesn't serve you.

I just had to do this myself. Someone who has worked as a part of my team for 10 years told me she landed a lucrative gig with a major sports organization. Inside I felt the pang of envy, wishing they were my client. I quickly snapped myself out of it with a mental slap. I had to remind myself that I want good things for my colleagues and their success does not negate mine in any way.

I was able to shift and respond in a way that felt good. I said, "Wow, that's amazing! How did you get that?" And then I listened intently. Because she had achieved something I could learn from. What did she do that I too could do to land a client like that? I ended up helping her by supplying an assessment tool and some content. It turned into a collaboration and I financially benefited from the gig too. Had I not been able to shift, I may not have been open to the possibility that followed. By remaining open and seeing opportunity, rather than competition, I ended up becoming a part of it.

The trick is to allow yourself to feel what you feel and not punish yourself for it. Don't berate yourself for a momentary and natural reaction. Instead, feel it and then overcome it by shifting back into an abundant mindset. If your colleague got a promotion that you were gunning for yourself, you are not going to instantly feel happy for them. You have to process the entirety of how you feel about that outcome. Release the emotions, privately or with a trusted confidant. Then break out the timer. In my house, we have a kitchen timer in the shape of a duck that quacks when the time is up. I used it with my kids when they were younger and whiny or having a meltdown. I would ask how many minutes they needed and together we would set the timer. Then I told them to let it all out. Until time is up, they (and you) have permission to wallow.

Give yourself the freedom to feel what you feel; throw yourself a pity party. Set the timer and when the duck quacks, it is time to shift. Then focus on whatever happiness you can muster for your colleague. Think about how their promotion may influence your next opportunity. Perhaps they're someone you already work well with, and you can talk to them about your own path. Or you can ask if you can help them with a plum assignment. If that is a stretch, focus on the next opportunity for you, because there will be one. Maybe this is the time to look for a fresh gig in a different department or even a different company.

There is a world of abundant opportunity out there for you! Think about what good can come from the momentary setback. I started this book with my story of getting laid off. It sucked, it hurt, and it felt like, "Why me?" But I will tell you that that's when my life started. That's when I started to discover what I was truly meant to do. It was life's way of saying, "You're not on the right path, and if you're not getting off, we're going to kick you off so you can find the correct path."

Practice Gratitude

Gratitude is strongly correlated with optimism, the cornerstone of an abundant mindset. There are numerous studies that outline the myriad benefits of gratitude, from enhancing empathy and improving self-esteem to feeling happier and even living longer. A practice of gratitude can help you access abundant thinking.

Practicing gratitude entails creating a habit that you can execute in whatever way that works for you. When I was growing up, my dad, a real estate agent, would go to houses and take Polaroids for the listings and my sister and I would be bored in the back seat. Some kids learn about the stars or cars. I learned about houses. And I never forgot. Once I moved into a house of my own, I found myself staring at other houses as I drove around. I think, often out loud, about what I like and don't like about them and compare them to the house that I have.

One day, my husband asked, "Why do you do that?" I told him that I never expected to have a house like we have, never expected to have the life we have. I am so grateful. I reminded him that the house I grew up in had rooms with no furniture and the furniture we did have was from the side of the road or Goodwill. He nodded, knowing my mom still loves to shop the "sidewalk sale." When I'm looking at other houses and comparing them to mine, I explained, it was my way of practicing gratitude for what I have.

Every day I ask my kids, "What was the best part of your day?" to get them in the habit of focusing on the good. Practicing gratitude can be infectious. Fostering gratitude in others is a way to practice it yourself. People who nurture gratitude and encourage it in others increase their likability and productive energy. The research corroborates this, stating that gratitude increases your energy level and not only helps you make friends, but deepens those relationships.

Gratitude journaling is a method that works for many. You don't have to wait until something particularly significant happens to feel gratitude. Simply writing, "I am thankful for my neighbor who always greets me with a smile and a wave" can instantly create a mental shift that generates a positive outlook. Take five minutes to write something you are grateful for every day. As your journal fills, you'll discover that you are very rarely writing the same thing twice. Taking the time every day to reflect on even the smallest moments for which you can be grateful will bolster an abundant mindset.

Invest Time

One thing we feel there is never enough of is time. It is true that time is one of the scarcest resources. Yet one of the best things you can do as a Connector is invest your time. It doesn't cost a thing, and it can lead to *so much*. The trick is to find the underused time of the day or week. Research shows that after 4 p.m. productivity levels drop significantly. And that Friday is the least productive day of the week.[2] Put those two facts together and Friday after 4 p.m. is a great time to invest in connections, since the work isn't getting done!

Your commute is another opportunity for found time. Since no one seems to talk to the people around them anymore and everyone is glued to their devices, reach out to someone virtually and put that commuting time to good use. If you are driving, connect your Bluetooth and a good conversation may make the traffic more bearable. For me, right after lunch, before the food digests, I enter a food coma and my brain shuts off. That is the time I like to catch up with someone on the phone since that reenergizes me. You have to know your energy highs and lows and use them to find extra time. Review the Law of Energy in chapter 4 of *The 11 Laws of Likability* to assess your energy knowledge. If you'd rather tackle following up with contacts between 8 and 9 a.m. before your coffee kicks in, go for it. You have to find what works for you, block off a time on your calendar and make it happen. Perhaps you devote 15 minutes to connecting each Thursday afternoon. That's fine—you can connect with a lot of people in 15 minutes! Now, I realize there are only 24 hours in every day, and we all need some downtime. Find the balance, but still extend yourself.

MINDSET MISSION
Invest Time

Think of five people you want to reach out to this week. Give yourself a reason to make it easier to follow through. It doesn't have to be an earth-shatteringly good reason. It could just be "You popped into my mind and I thought I would check in."

In person: Who: _____   Reason: _____

Phone call: Who: _____   Reason: _____

Email: Who: _____   Reason: _____

Video chat: Who: _____   Reason: _____

_____: Who: _____   Reason: _____

Now reach out. Then think of five people you want to reach out to next week. Keep a list going in your calendar of people you want to reach out to. I have a list of people in NYC that I want to connect with live. When I plan a city day, I reach out to see if we can get together. It can be as easy as saying, "Hey, I'm going to be in your neighborhood this Wednesday; are you around?" Even if you don't get together, you've come to the front of their mind and kept the connection alive.

Choose your channel to connect. Email is the least invasive but also the least responsive and easiest to ignore. The most proximate channel for connection is face-to-face, but Skype is a great backup. Next most proximate are phone calls, then text/instant chat. They have a speed of response that aren't usually found via email. If you're unsure of the other person's interest, choose the least proximate channel—email—to initiate. I'll sometimes follow up with a voicemail if I'm worried my email tone may be misconstrued.

If you are wondering if there are better times of the day or week than others, my answer is it depends. I have one client who works in government, and between 5 and 6 p.m. is the sweet spot. He's just too busy during the day to ever pick up my call. Occasionally, I'll try

8 a.m. with corporate clients. If they are early birds, often their assistant isn't in yet and they pick up the phone. I personally don't feel that there's a bad time of year to make a connection. Sometimes even the holidays are a great time to meet for coffee.

If you are not yet convinced connecting is worth the investment of time, perhaps Kristen Pressner can change your mind. She is the global head of human resources for a $12-billion and 35,000-person diagnostics company, the mother of four, and the sole breadwinner for her family. She is one busy lady, yet still found time for an interview for this book. She shares, "I spend 50% of my time investing in relationships that will remove 80% of my work later." When pressed on the statistic, she explains, "Connecting with a wide range of people is in the 'important but not urgent box.' It is a leap of faith that the payback—as obscure and unsure as it feels now—will come and it's a good investment. I've always found this to be true." Me too, Kristen, which is why I am writing this book!

Making Time for Connections

Juggling all the demands on your time is something everyone struggles with. I don't think balance exists, but choices do. We can all make choices about what we want to fit in and what we don't. The bigger challenge is how. So I reached out to Dorie Clark, author of *Entrepreneurial You*; *Reinventing You*; and *Stand Out*; and adjunct professor at Duke University's Fuqua School of Business (DorieClark.com). She receives daily requests for her time and still prioritizes connecting.

She shares, "As you become more successful, inevitably there's a shift: instead of having to petition others to meet with you, people start to seek you out. At first, that can be enormously flattering. But as you get busier, you realize that while a certain amount of 'non-strategic' networking is a mitzvah, it can quickly derail your productivity and ability to accomplish your own work." She shares three tips for fitting it all in.

1. **Use content creation as a first pass.** Dorie has a simple way to deal with requests from people who haven't done their homework before reaching out. If they ask a question already answered in her articles or books, she simply refers them to the resource in lieu of meeting with them. You may be thinking this doesn't apply to you, but it could. With the access and ease of technology today, anyone can create content via blog posts, articles, videos, or podcasts to answer the questions you hear most often. Alternatively, if you are the go-to person for something, help develop another go-to person. Consider the other resources and other routes to get the information they seek from you.

2. **Combine networking meetings with your existing schedule.** Much of the time, people are just seeking to initiate or extend contact without a specific question. Rather than making time for individual sit-downs with everyone, Dorie suggests you think about events you're already scheduled to attend (like a charity event or professional association gathering) or activities you're already planning to do (such as take a class at the gym). Perhaps you can invite your new contact to that event and multitask. I often meet someone right after a workout at a diner. After all, I have to eat. (I do warn them I will be sweaty.)

3. **Host group gatherings.** This is my favorite Dorie-ism. I was honored and admittedly a little confused, the first time I was invited to what I fondly call Dorie's Dinners. She frequently hosts group dinner gatherings and invites new contacts as well as those she wants to stay connected with to all attend. She is not buying a room full of people dinner. She picks a place willing to give separate checks so everyone has the freedom to leave when they need to. As Dorie explains, "This provides a great way to get to know

someone casually—and to see if I'd like to deepen the connection later—and also provides value to them, because they're meeting multiple new people in addition to me." It is also extremely efficient, if you ask me. Now she cohosts dinners to expand her network and we are planning one together soon.

Now I am not unrealistic: I get it, I have a graveyard of business cards on my desk. You can't reach out to and follow up with everyone, so don't. I give you permission to *not* follow up with everyone. Be selective. Stretch out the frequency with which you touch base with and nurture your network. It is okay to position yourself as the recipient of the reach-out and leave the initiative to the other person sometimes. I will never be able to reach out to all the people who hand me a card, but if you email me, you will always get a response. It comes down to this: don't say you will if you are not sure you will. An action stated and not executed erodes credibility. We're all busy, and it's not always easy to make time to build and maintain new connections. With these strategies, you can take control of your schedule and therefore be more likely to enjoy the connections you do make.

CONNECTORS DON'T act from a place of fear or scarcity, rather they believe in abundant opportunities for all. They give credit to others and don't feel like they're in competition with anyone but themselves. They believe that things don't just happen to you—you *make* them happen. Abundance begets abundance.

Refresh
Your Memory

Abundance is what a Connector believes in: an abundance of opportunities, an abundance of work, and an abundance of relationships.

Acknowledge the fear. Scarcity is understandably scary. To overcome scarce thinking, acknowledge and seek to understand the source of the fear.

Trust yourself, your skills, and your value to build internal confidence and access abundant thinking. Stop judging yourself in relation to other people.

Give credit. When you shine the light on someone else, it reflects back on you. Look for opportunities to credit others.

Practice gratitude by focusing on the positive. Encouraging the practice of gratitude in others propels abundant thinking.

Be motivated by others. Coming from a place of abundance doesn't mean you never have moments of envy. Use the feeling not to be competitive with them, but to be motivated by them.

Invest time—it's one of the best things you can do as a Connector. Find the underused time of the day or week when you're less productive on work and use it to connect.

7

Connectors Trust

*"The best way to find out if you
can trust somebody is to trust them."*

ERNEST HEMINGWAY

There Is No Connection without Trust

Trust is at the core of a Connector: the ability to trust yourself, the inclination to trust others, and the potential to be trusted by others. But what exactly is trust? *Webster's Dictionary* defines trust as "assured reliance on the character, ability, strength, or truth of someone or something." An alternative definition is the confident expectation of something, hope. I like that one, as hope is an indication of faith or belief without proof.

Trust is this amorphous concept that we all know but each of us may define it a little differently. To me, trust is having confidence in a person to complete a task, and it's how you expect someone to respond to a given situation. It's unwavering and consistent. To explore what trust is, I took the question to my training programs. During a module on building trust, I ask a group to write a definition of the word. I have overheard participants discuss the idea from the noun, verb, and adjective angles and struggle to define it. At the end, they always come up with a definition, but I have *never* gotten the same definition twice. Two have always stuck with me:

1. Trust is the expectation of predictability.
2. Trust is a feeling or connection that creates a bond rooted in certainty, reliability, and consistency. There is no timeline for creation or destruction. It is fluid.

I love that: **trust is fluid.** I think it is also situational. I trust my dog to let me know if there's someone breaking into my house, but I do *not* trust my dog to not eat my food if I leave it unattended. We have different levels and types of trust with different people in different situations.

When you are connecting with someone, your bond grows stronger and deeper along with your knowledge of the other person and how your interactions will flow with them. We all have that one friend we know we'll love seeing a certain movie with, and another one we call when we want to go shopping, and another we'll chat about work with. Because of the trust we've built up in the relationship over a period of time, we know which friend will give us candid feedback on a career issue, or have advice for child rearing, or job searching, and so on. Without the faith you have in the person and your relationship, you wouldn't be reaching out to them. You wouldn't open up. Bottom line—**there is no connection without trust.**

You Must Trust Yourself First

Self-trust is not dissimilar to self-esteem, or inner confidence, a quality my research showed was felt at a higher rate in Connectors. We are all familiar with the saying, "Trust your gut." For those who rely more on facts and data, trusting your gut can be uncomfortable. On top of that, we must overcome our formative years, relying on peers, parents, and pop culture to form opinions on right and wrong, cool and uncool. We spend so much of our life evaluating how we *should* act, how we *should* feel, and what decisions we *should* make from the perspective of other people. As a result, it is hard to separate *our* opinions from the opinions that surround us.

Cultivating positive connections will bolster self-trust. Many of us have toxic relationships that we may not realize are eroding our self-trust. I had a friend in college who was always there for me, always offered to drop everything if I asked. I never asked. I didn't need someone to be extreme, so it didn't occur to me to offer to be extreme for her. But when I didn't offer, she deemed me a terrible friend. I was always questioning if I was being a good enough friend, worried about her assessment of me. I was on eggshells and the friendship didn't last. Reduce your exposure to the toxic relationships in your life. Spend time with people who are reinforcing and resilient. You become more like those who you spend the most time with.

Self-trust stems from an increased awareness of what you are thinking and feeling and not just to what you are doing. It is a critical success factor in your career and work. It is the ability to share your knowledge and allow others to experience the real you. When you trust yourself, you listen to your inner wisdom and don't minimize what you know. Trusting yourself is a learned skill. It is a habit that will become muscle memory. When you don't trust yourself, you can hardly expect that others would be able to trust you. So start with yourself.

MINDSET MISSION
Increase Your Self-Trust

Just as gratitude journaling can help bolster an abundant mindset, acknowledgment tracking can build the muscle of self-trust. A few questions can prompt your mind to recognize what you do well and bring it to the surface. Make a daily practice of answering a few of the acknowledgment opportunities listed below. You do not need to do all of them every day. Allow yourself the empathy you'd extend to another. Find your habit.

1. What is one thing I did well today?
2. I am proud that I _____.
3. Today I accomplished _____.
4. I had a good encounter with _____.
5. I overcame it when _____ happened.
6. I felt good about myself when _____.
7. I had a positive impact on _____ (person or situation).

The Four Pillars of Trust

I talk a lot about being aware of how people perceive you, building your personal brand, and becoming clear on how you want to be known. It starts with that instant assessment someone makes of you. But that is (*hopefully*) just the beginning of a relationship. If you want to create a lasting connection, what makes the difference is the long-term perception that the other person has of you. Your lasting brand is built on the belief that what they know and expect about you is what they get. It's the promise of the experience they will have when interacting with you. Relationships are about trust—because **trust is the foundation of connection.**

So how do you infuse trust into the impression you are making? In my work, I have identified four fundamental aspects of trust which I call the pillars of trust: **Authenticity, Vulnerability, Transparency,** and **Consistency.** Each of these pillars is an integral part of building and maintaining trust with those around you, and none can be neglected.

1. Authenticity

The first Law of Likability is that the *real* you is the best you. That doesn't mean we don't flex and adjust to enable connections with one another. It *does* mean that we stop acting like we think others want us to. There is no "work persona"—there is only you. You have to be willing to share some information about yourself, because if you are not bringing the real you, there's no ability to connect or trust. The Connector mindset of being open and accepting will enable authentic interactions and is the foundation for trust.

2. **Vulnerability**

Vulnerability used to be a completely offensive idea to me. After all, who wants to be vulnerable? If I am vulnerable, I am leaving myself open to being hurt or taken advantage of. People will think I am weak. Any of those thoughts resonate with you? I get it. It took a long time to realize that **vulnerability is not weakness; it's openness.** Vulnerability means self-disclosure, acknowledging your mistakes, and being okay with being imperfect. Vulnerability leads to credibility. Which would you rather a manager who criticizes you when you admit a mistake or a manager who takes the moment to share a similar experience they went through or a time when they messed up and how they recovered from it? Allowing others to see behind the curtain is being vulnerable. Using your experiences to teach allows others to learn from you and establishes credibility, connection, and trust.

3. **Transparency**

BusinessDictionary.com defines transparency as the lack of hidden agendas accompanied by the availability of full information required for collaboration, cooperation, and collective decision-making. Transparent leadership is key to creating a culture of trust between leaders and their employees. When employees are kept in the loop and understand their role in the overarching purpose and goals of the company, they are more engaged and have greater trust in their employer. It comes down to this: if you don't share information, people will come up with their own answers to their questions. They will spin their own stories, which will rarely be the ones you *want* them to be. Keep people in the loop even if you don't have all the answers, and they will trust that you will tell them when you do.

4. **Consistency**

To be consistent is to act the same way over time. Consistency is the cornerstone of trust. If trust is an expectation of predictability, that cannot exist without consistency—since that expectation and belief is formed through experience. At the end of the day, all of these aspects are needed, but they won't matter unless you demonstrate authenticity, vulnerability, and transparency on a regular basis. They are not just do-it-once concepts. You have to consistently apply these four pillars time after time in order to build and maintain trust.

Trust: How We Build It, Break It, and Restore It

According to my survey results, most people are neutral on giving trust freely. It needs to be earned, and it needs to be built. Connectors are slightly more likely (1.4 times) to trust other people's honesty than Non-Connectors. To enhance your ability to build and maintain trust with others, it is important to analyze how trust is built, broken, and restored in organizations.

How to Build Trust

Trust can be built between two people as well as between a person and a company. Individuals build trust by incorporating the four pillars into their interactions and behavior. Some measures that build trust include: following through on what you say you'll do, not asking others to do things you wouldn't do yourself, modeling the behavior you seek in others, giving credit, acknowledging contributions, being honest, keeping confidences, sharing information, having a person's back, and empowering others to act.

For an organization, the mechanisms for building trust are not that different. To cultivate an environment of trust, the organizational culture should include: regular and robust communication from leadership, sufficient resources, reasonable workloads, flexible schedules for work–life balance, realistic goals and expectations, and fair rewards.

There is a correlation between the first two weeks on the job and the longevity on that job. How a new employee is on-boarded will impact their feelings about the organization from day one. And it is well established how difficult it is to change that first impression. I will never forget my first day at my first job after college. I chose the now defunct Arthur Andersen and negotiated three items before signing on the dotted line: working for the manager who'd recruited me, being assigned a casino as a client, and recruiting at my undergraduate university. When I received my schedule, none of those items were included. The first response to my inquiry was a patronizing, "You don't always get what you want." Disillusioned was an understatement. Needless to say, my trust was shattered and my tenure was short. Building trust should be thought about in every interaction and every company policy.

How We Break Trust

Trust is not something that we think about every day. As a result, we don't realize the things we are doing that break the trust of those around us. There are some obvious ways trust is broken: intentional and often unintentional lying; breaking a promise or commitment; not doing what you said you would do; cheating; not taking responsibility; stealing ideas, information, or credit; and throwing others under the bus. I am sure you could add to the list as you recall how someone betrayed you.

During a training program, I posed the question, "How is trust broken in organizations?" and a participant responded nonchalantly with, "Spying." I made a confused, questioning face at her and blurted, "What do you mean? Spying?!" I thought, "That doesn't really happen, does it?" She replied, "You know... 'Be my eyes and ears,'" and suddenly I understood. People use this phrase all the time. But that doesn't make the actual practice correct. We often do things that we think are just a part of the way the business world works— but really these things are eroding the trust of the people around us.

There is also a laundry list of seemingly innocuous ways that trust is broken: withholding or hoarding information, gossiping, being inconsiderate or disrespectful, dismissing something someone feels is important, keeping secrets, white lies, covering up mistakes, micromanaging, sending mixed messages, shutting down others' ideas, revealing private information due to carelessness. Have you ever sent an email and included someone you shouldn't have? I was mortified when I forwarded an email where I had a private exchange about the other person's health. I had forgotten the email chain had that information when I used it to respond to a larger group. I apologized profusely and we moved past it. Unintentional or not, it still happened and damaged the trust we were building.

Be vigilant and tune into how other people's actions impact your level of trust. Then check yourself for those subtle ways you may be breaking the trust of those in your circle and adjust.

How to Restore Trust

It is possible, though difficult, to restore trust once it's broken, and if you don't at least try, you'll never accomplish it. Rebuilding trust doesn't just happen. It takes a willingness by both parties. The first step in restoring trust is apologizing and accepting responsibility for your actions. Be clear on your desire to restore that trust. Acknowledging what you did wrong and communicating your understanding of why it was wrong will help.

It is a tricky thing to ask the hurt party, "What can I do to make it better?" as that puts the onus on them to figure out a solution. Take that on yourself. Share how you intend to act differently going forward. Explain what you learned from the incident and how you plan to prevent a recurrence. Once you establish your intended efforts, you can then ask, "Is there anything else you would like to have happen?" Have a plan to hold yourself accountable. When you say what you will do, you then have to do it and not just one time. It can be hard to stick with the plan when you continue to feel the distrust of the other person. Remember, trust is not rebuilt with one corrected behavior. It takes consistently showing a new course of action.

As part of the process, expect an emotional or angry response. Allow the person to vent and release their feelings about what you did. Don't defend or explain. Just listen. In the end, part of restoring trust is forgiving yourself and allowing yourself to let go and move forward. Don't give up on your desire to restore trust. Don't expect overnight results. Like anything worth doing, it takes time.

Trust Needs to Be Given to Be Received

My father is a self-made man who never went to college. He grew up very poor and taught me to always think about how others could take advantage of me so I could prevent it. That is how he saw the world, perhaps as a result of his experiences. One of his first jobs was in a used car lot. The owners taught him how to dig grooves in tires; he later realized it was to make them look newer to match the odometer they had rolled back. When I was car shopping, he made sure I knew how to test the accuracy of the mileage, check the oil levels, and know if automatic fluid was the right color. He knew the likelihood of being swindled, so he thought and sought to prevent what he expected.

On the flip side, my mother always taught me to trust someone until or unless they gave you a reason not to. I adopted her philosophy and prefer to approach people with the idea that they're trustworthy. It is definitely a choice and not my natural inclination. By placing trust and confidence in others, you often reap the benefit of being trusted yourself. In my line of work, I have to trust that others aren't going to steal my clients. How do I ensure that's not going to happen? I can't! I just have to trust the people I choose to put in front of my clients. So while my dad may have taught me how to be skeptical and cynical, my choice is to be trusting and put relationships first.

I'm not saying you should just blindly trust every person. You don't have to trust a person in every scenario but instead for one certain thing. You can be selective. Maybe you trust your colleague to get the job done, but you do not trust them to keep a secret, because they tend to gossip. Trust your own intuition—those butterflies in your gut—about who to rely on for each issue on your short list.

The good news is the survey results revealed you don't have to have a natural propensity to trust to be a Connector; they have a slight innate tendency toward trust, but not an overwhelming one. So if you feel you tend not to have a trusting personality, that doesn't prevent you from adopting a trusting mindset. The behaviors within this mindset can be learned.

YOU CAN still make casual acquaintances without the critical component of trust, but you'll never get to that place of a full connection without it. Be aware of and prevent those actions that can erode the trust of those around you. You have to give trust to receive trust. Show your colleagues and employees that you believe in them. Empower others around you, and you may just see that trust returned.

Refresh
Your Memory

Trust is at the core of a Connector: the ability to trust yourself, the inclination to trust others, and the potential to be trusted by others.

Trust is the expectation of predictability.

The four pillars of trust are:

1. **Authenticity:** *You have to be willing to share some information about yourself. If you are not bringing the real you, there's no way to connect or trust.*

2. **Vulnerability:** *Vulnerability means self-disclosure, acknowledging your mistakes, and being okay with being imperfect. Vulnerability leads to credibility.*

3. **Transparency:** *Keep people in the loop even if you don't have all the answers, and they will trust that you will tell them when you do.*

4. **Consistency:** *To be consistent is to act the same way over time. Consistency is the cornerstone of trust.*

Restore trust. We do things daily to build and break trust. Restore broken trust over time. Start by apologizing and accepting responsibility. Acknowledging the impact and establishing a plan of action will lay the foundation for future trust.

8

Connectors Are Social and Curious

"You can make more friends in two months by becoming really interested in other people than you can in two years by trying to get other people interested in you. Which is just another way of saying that the way to make a friend is to be one."

DALE CARNEGIE

We Are All Social Beings

To be social is simply to seek or enjoy companionship of others. It is not, by definition, being a social butterfly or the life of the party—in fact, in my survey, I found that doesn't matter whatsoever when it comes to someone's status as a Connector. Being social does not require you to enjoy large groups of people; it just means you like being part of and interacting with a community of people. We are all social beings, but that does not mean interactions with others don't exhaust us at times, even the extroverts.

Although people are often classified as either **introvert** (drained by social encounters and energized by solitary activities) or **extrovert** (energized by being around other people), the truth is that many of us are "ambiverts" (occasionally called "omniverts")—people whose personality has a balance of both features. **Ambiverts** are either introverts who enjoy socializing from time to time or extroverts who need some time alone after socializing. No matter how you classify yourself, it won't determine your efficacy or abilities to connect as a social being. I want you to embrace being social in a way that works for *you*. You'll connect better when you do what's authentic for you: as I found in my survey results, 94% of Connectors strongly agree that when communicating with others, they try to be genuine with what they say and do. They weren't exclusively introverts or extroverts; they were both. We are all social beings with a need for connection. How we connect with others is up to each of us—there is no one or right way.

Find Your Format

Shocking news, but not everyone loves networking events—milling about by the hors d'oeuvres table to strike up conversations with people you have never met. I admit it, even as an extrovert, sometimes I find those events extremely draining. I have to psych myself up for them and harness my energy to enter that daunting room with the right mindset. You may be relieved to hear my research revealed that Connectors do not have to be social in a traditional or extroverted way. It's the same concept as "find your tribe," only in this instance, it is **find your format**. Even the most extroverted person may feel unsure in some social settings or in the virtual world where there is not always feedback. Being social is more a matter of pinpointing what works for you.

In today's technology-reliant society, there are now more ways than ever to be social. You can interact with other individuals or groups without leaving the comfort and security of your home. Consider the three main mechanisms for socialization: virtual, group, and one-on-one. Within each of these main approaches, you can further refine your preferred format for interacting. Being social can look different for everyone. If you do not like groups, don't go to large events all the time. I would, however, encourage you to go sometimes. It is important to find your format and also to stretch yourself. Increase your ability and comfort with other formats to increase your confidence when you do have to navigate those social settings.

Group Settings

Group settings are often the most challenging, even for the most outwardly social people. There are many benefits to these types of events that you should consider before crossing this option off your list:

- They enable you to select a group with similar interests, job function, work challenge, or professional industry. With preestablished commonalities, conversations of interest are easier to uncover.
- You can meet many people at the same time and increase your probability of finding people you connect with.
- There are frequent opportunities to attend these types of events and hone your connecting skills in a lower-risk setting.

Introverts might consider approaching networking events differently—perhaps get there early, when everyone is looking for someone to talk to. You can volunteer to work the desk or be a greeter, giving you an assigned role and therefore an easy excuse to strike up a conversation. Keep in mind the dos and don'ts for a group setting, outlined in Figure 8.1.

Figure 8.1: The Dos and Don'ts of Group Settings

DO	DON'T
Smile	Have closed-off or uninviting body language
Make eye contact	Stare at your phone
Keep your body slightly open, not shoulder to shoulder	Close off the circle too tight
Enable others to join your group conversation	Make it difficult for others to break in to your group
Introduce yourself to new members	Ignore new members of the group
Approach individuals who are on their own	Be afraid to approach and invite a person to join

Virtual Connecting

There are so many ways to connect and build relationships without ever leaving your home or office: social media, video chat, or online groups. (I go in depth about a few of the options in part III.) The best tip I can give you is not just to join but to participate if you want to create connections. Social media can be overwhelming—there are so many sites that can suck your time. Think about where the people you want to connect with hang out online. Consider joining groups that are of professional as well as personal interest. And don't be afraid to turn on that video camera. Putting a face to a voice and being able to read body language immediately creates a stronger bond than just audio and certainly more than text or email.

One-on-One Interactions

Whether via video or face-to-face, remember that connecting happens one-on-one. Live opportunities don't have to be planned or professional. Honestly, it is often easier to engage your social side out of the office. Social connections happen often in unlikely places, like at the dog park, in the line at the restroom, or in the stands at a sports event. Last year, during a field trip for my son's class, another mother mentioned she was in a working women's affinity group and would love to talk to me about speaking there. We were both chaperones on a trip and it naturally bridged to business. Connections happen when they aren't forced. Lasting connections happen every day at places of worship, mahjong and poker tables, book and knitting clubs, running groups, charity events... The goal is to find a format that works for you and attend regularly.

Often reconnecting and resurrecting friendships from the past to the present can create some of the strongest bonds. Especially if that shared past is pleasant. I told you about my sister's introduction to the head of NBC's digital publishing, someone she dated in junior high. At our first meeting, I brought him a picture I had of him in seventh grade wearing a yellow baseball shirt tucked into high-waisted gray sweatpants! (I think he thought it was still the '70s!) Leveraging a shared past kicked off the current connection.

Create, Join, or Volunteer

I receive a ton of emails every day. I often delete ones from various alumni clubs or networking groups without much more than a skim. So why don't I just get off the list? Because once in a while I see an event that I am glad to attend. Sometimes I'll share it with someone else and not personally attend.

Recently it was an all alumni ski trip that caught my eye. A man named Fred was organizing it for the sixth year, and I wondered why it was the first year I had heard about it. I registered my family to join, and it was a great trip with alumni of all ages—but I noticed Fred wasn't skiing. Curious, I asked him why he organized the trip if he wasn't going to enjoy it. His first response was, "I love to throw a good party." He then shared the impetus for the original trip—to create a community of alumni from his alma mater—and how even when that purpose evaporated, he continued because of the people.

Fred built relationships with every single person there. People came year after year because of him. I asked if he ever did business with anyone from the trip. He responded, "Yes, but that's not why I do it." He added, "If I go looking for a lead, I can't find one," but on the trip, it seems to just happen.

Fred's ski weekend is a great example of creating an event. Though his original impetus was building a network of alumni from his alma mater, the event expanded to include multiple schools. Relationships form faster when you have the built-in association of a person, community, or experience. There are tons of events already out there, both large and small, but if you find what you are looking for doesn't exist, then create it.

Create a Community

A community provides a feeling of fellowship with others as a result of sharing common attitudes, interests, and goals. Who do you want to be in a community with? There are multiple ways to kick-start new groups; they can be in person or online or a mix between the two.

Here are a few examples of people who created the community they wanted. Perhaps one has your people already and you can simply join.

Network Under 40: When a friend asked Darrah Brustein, "Where do you suggest I go to make friends after college?" she couldn't think of a good answer, so she founded an organization that would intersect friendship and business. She created a peer-to-peer environment where relationships come before transactions. Launched in Atlanta in 2011, Network Under 40 (NetworkUnder40.com) now serves 30,000-plus young professionals in six U.S. cities and counting.

Ivy: When Beri Meric left Harvard Business School, he missed the tribe of like-minded folks he met there. He solved the problem by cofounding Ivy (Ivy.com), the Social University, which is creating collegiate-inspired communities in cities across the globe.

Intern Queen: Anyone who has ever been an intern knows that it is not easy when you're at the bottom of the ladder. Lauren Berger launched the website Intern Queen (InternQueen.com) in 2009 in an effort to help connect worthy would-be interns with desirable positions. The result? Lauren created a hub for recent graduates that her future clients want access to. Creating a community to benefit the members turned into a business with endless benefits for all.

Young Entrepreneur Council (YEC): Scott Gerber promised himself if he ever succeeded, he would work to ensure that no young entrepreneur ever felt alone or struggled without the proper resources. With cofounder Ryan Paugh, they created the Young Entrepreneur Council (YEC.co) to empower young entrepreneurs who believe that doing well and doing good are not mutually exclusive.

GirlFriend Circles: This online community was started by Shasta Nelson—a friendship expert who wrote the book *Frientimacy: How to Deepen Friendships for Lifelong Health and Happiness.* GirlFriend Circles (GirlFriendCircles.com) is a safe and encouraging place to ask for advice, meet other women in your area who want to meet new friends, share experiences, and keep on learning about the research that supports building better relationships.

Create an Event

Sometimes creating and curating a community may seem like a bigger challenge and commitment than you want to take on. So start small and create an event within your network, whether it's hosting an annual Cinco de Mayo party or having monthly dinners with the same group of friends. It can be a one-time thing or recurring gathering. If you are worried about cost, don't. Design a gathering that either doesn't cost anything or where people pay their way.

Start small and maybe your event will transform into a community. That is what happened for Rebecca Friese Rodskog, founder of an invite-only Bay Area luncheon for 12 hand-selected women that she calls 12@12. Rebecca, first mentioned in chapter 1, firmly believes that magic happens when the right women come together, so she creates the space to enable those connections.

Join and Find Your People

If you don't want to create your own event or group, find one that suits you. The fact is, there are likely hundreds, if not thousands, of them near your home. When I first moved to the suburbs, I joined an online group for moms, then I found a mom-owned business group that met locally. As my personal and professional needs changed, so did the groups I belonged to. I am a huge fan of the Nextdoor platform (Nextdoor.com), a private social network allowing you to stay up on what's going on in your neighborhood. You can recommend doctors and plumbers, post events, send direct messages, and sell to those in your and nearby neighborhoods.

Seek both personal and professional networks. I joined a local chapter of the National Speakers Association and gained friends, mentors, and strategic partners all in one place. The best group I ever joined has to be Authoress, an online community of female authors created by Denise Brosseau and Sarah Granger. I have referenced the group throughout the book as so many contributed their expertise and introductions. "Getting a book out is hard, and sharing great ideas is a journey," Sarah explains. "This network is a warning signal, resource provider, and safety valve for conversation. It has become an amplifier."

Sarah approached Denise who she knew from the Forum for Women Entrepreneurs, a trade association Denise had founded, and reached out through her website (ThoughtLeadershipLab.com). Denise is a serial community builder and joiner who believes in the power of community to change the world. Together, they started the Authoress group by inviting a dozen women they knew in the San Francisco Bay Area who had published books to connect through a Google group. Today, the group has more than 220 members across the country and a few international members. The only way into the group is by invitation from a current member.

Groups can be open, invitation only, paid, or even require an application. BNI is an example of a formal networking group requiring both an application and a fee. The mission of BNI is to help members increase their business through a structured, positive, and professional referral marketing program that enables them to develop long-term, meaningful relationships with quality business professionals.

I have always known about BNI and had been invited to be a guest at meetings in the past. I hadn't joined because of the timing of meetings and level of commitment required at a time when I had small kids. When I attended a recent meeting, I realized BNI was the perfect organization to highlight and went about trying to connect with the right person to get permission. What happens when you are a Connector? I mentioned interest during an interview with a podcaster and was told to use his name to reach out to BNI's founder, Ivan Misner. You know how the story ends: Ivan not only replied with permission and an interview, he wrote the foreword to this book! Ivan truly understands and values the impact of connection.

Volunteer and Connect through Cause

Volunteering results in some of the strongest and often unlikely connections. I told you in chapter 5 that by chairing an animal rescue event, I landed my first client, JP Morgan. Kristen Lamoreaux, founder of SIM (Society for Information Management) Women, a networking organization for female CIOs and their direct reports, calls it *networking through philanthropy*: "When you are giving away some of your precious free time for a cause you truly believe in, you are not there for the sale, you are there for the greater good. Yet simply being present allows you to connect with people on a genuine level, regardless of their title, position, or company."

Trust is built more quickly in philanthropic situations. It's not surprising, when everyone is there to do good. There are shared values and interest, so trust forms more easily. "The key is to put the cause first and networking second," shares Kristen. "A salesperson might join a charitable organization with a noted CEO on its board in hopes of scoring some face-time during a fundraising event. But such superficial interactions won't generate any traction." Instead, Kristen recommends volunteering consistently with a nonprofit you truly care to help.

That is exactly what Eric Gorham did when he cofounded the Gateway to Innovation Conference (G2IConference.com) to make a difference for schools in St. Louis, Missouri. The organization invests in the technology needs of schools, STEM programs, and children themselves. Attendees and sponsors get involved and devote time and resources and use their networks all because they share the goal to strengthen the community. "The network I built from a business side is huge," he tells me. Eric has hired people and also referred people he volunteered with. "My association with the conference has opened doors," Eric professes. When St. Louis government agencies were experiencing denial of service attacks, Eric was able to call the CIOs of two major organizations to help work the problem—simply because of the connections he had made through the event. Sincere involvement with an organization you care about can help you build solid, long-lasting relationships with your fellow volunteers.

The Introvert's Edge

When I reached out to my network asking for stories of Connectors, I received an email from a longtime friend introducing me to Cindy.

Lily wrote, "Cindy is a wonderful person who creates meaningful relationships with everyone she comes in contact with. She is also so giving and is always looking for ways to connect people she knows for personal or professional reasons. I simply adore her."

Cindy took a while to reply to the introduction, explaining, "It didn't immediately resonate why so many people refer to me as a Connector." Lily shared that Cindy would describe herself as "an introvert, a really good listener." That made perfect sense to me as listening is key to finding the opportunities and commonalities.

What really resonates for me in her email is when she wrote, "I don't usually think about making connections for personal gains, but more because I've uncovered a fit."

"That, Cindy," I replied, "is a Connector mindset." We had a long email exchange and I realized she thought extroversion was a prerequisite to being a Connector. I cleared up that misconception for her and want to disabuse anyone out there of that thinking.

One of the best Connectors I know is an introvert; it's the same Sarah who cofounded the Authoress group. Though I have never met Sarah in person, I have met many people through knowing her in a virtual format. Sarah is an author, speaker, and self-described introvert. She shares, "I felt socially awkward as a kid—less able to easily start conversations than other people. By high school, I generally felt more comfortable making friends and communicating online." She jokes about her introversion but is no longer phobic of social events. She does both, but excels in online connecting. As she put it, "I was good at identifying people with similar interests and inviting them to collaborate together online." You can read her digital dos and don'ts in chapter 11.

Matthew Pollard, host of *The Introvert's Edge* podcast (and my inspiration for the title of this section), believes that "introversion is something to be embraced, not overcome. You already have every talent and ability you need in order to outsell and out-network your extroverted counterparts. You just need to learn the systems and strategies to hone your inherent skills and translate them to business success."

Matthew hosted another podcaster on his show, Jaime Masters of *Eventual Millionaire*. While most think Jaime is an extrovert now, as a speaker and podcast host, she had a fairly strong form of introversion—she would turn blotchy red when she was nervous speaking with strangers. When she started her own business, she knew she had to overcome that to be successful. Initially she needed a push from her mentor but, over time, Jaime developed her own approach and thinking around building connections.

"One of the tactics that I've learned is just trying to make *them* feel comfortable," she says. She brings people to events so she can make introductions. She also shares a controversial tactic: "I hug people. It's one of those things where you can start making them feel more connected." Touching can be tricky and it is certainly easier for women than men, so use your judgment and recognize that touching an arm is much more acceptable than touching someone's back. Make the touch brief as a lingering touch can be awkward or misconstrued.

Finding points of commonality is what Jaime calls "connection threads," and she believes the more connection threads she makes when she meets someone, the higher her chances of creating a bond with them. Jaime explains, "At the beginning, it was me going, 'I just want to be your friend,' literally." I must admit I have used that same line when meeting someone I just wanted to know. While her tips might seem extreme, they work for her. She is now considered a pro networker. She shares, "I still turn red, I didn't get rid of that. But I'm not nervous as much and I'm over the fact that I turn red and I bring it up."

I repeat: **Connectors do not need to be extroverts!** Many introverts are amazing Connectors with their own way to do it. They leverage their natural listening skills to make people feel heard. They are able to focus their attention on the person in front of them. All of these innately introverted qualities are advantages when it comes to connection.

How to Work a Room

Networking events are a common and often dreaded means to make new connections. Those environments can be daunting even for the most comfortable networker. That's why I reached out to my friend Susan RoAne, author of the bestselling book *How to Work a Room* (SusanRoAne.com), for her top tips to navigate these events. If you want to learn more from Susan, she also authored *The Secrets of Savvy Networking*; *What Do I Say Next?*; and *How to Create Your Own Luck*.

- **Align Your Attitude.** Susan explains you need to "check your attitude and energy before attending an event. If you're going to show up, be positive, enthusiastic, and upbeat! People are attracted to others who are enjoying themselves." It also helps to consider why you are attending the event. She cautions, "Don't have an agenda. We can tell if you do. Be guided, not blinded, by your goals." I always say, if you don't have the right energy to be there, go home. I give you permission to skip an event and attend the next one. But make sure you don't give yourself the out too often. Stretch yourself.

- **Prepare for Conversation.** If you have a concern over how to start a conversation or what you will talk about, Susan advises that you "know what is going on in your profession, city, state, and the world. Prepare three to five items to interject, reference, or discuss." People relate more to stories than facts so she suggests you "check out the business and sports pages, trade journals, movie reviews, and your favorite content curators so that you have something to talk about." Those stories can make for great conversational anecdotes. My advice is to make sure you are actually interested in the topics, so the conversation can extend through natural interest and curiosity and not be forced.

- **Initiate Introductions.** Susan refers to name tags as "a gift of information and a source to start a conversation." Wear yours on the right-hand side so it is in the line of sight with an extended handshake. And as you extend your hand, she advises, "introduce yourself and use the person's name." If you have already met, reintroduce yourself and others will generally respond in kind. This is her trick to save everyone the embarrassment of forgotten names. If you want to wait for someone else to initiate, make eye contact and smile. It acts as an invitation and indicates approachability. You want to make it easy for people to talk to you.

- **Rescue Someone.** I call it the lone wolf. Susan says look for the white-knuckled drinker. Often there are people who are not in conversation and look uncomfortable in the environment. She describes them as having "the glass gripped so tightly for support that the knuckles turn white. That person, who is speaking to no one, would welcome your conversations." Go talk to them!

- **Attend with a Friend.** Susan recommends you choose someone in a non-competitive field so you can cross-promote each other: "Choose a companion who will introduce you with the same level of enthusiasm that you have demonstrated." There are mixed opinions on this one. Matthew Pollard, author of *The Introvert's Edge*, will tell you to go alone so you don't depend on someone else to make introductions. Ivan Misner, founder of BNI, suggested on Matthew's *Introvert's Edge* podcast that if you're an introvert, go with an extrovert who can introduce you all night. I think both approaches can work, but be aware of the drawbacks of each.

- **Extricate Graciously.** I agree fully with Susan that knowing how to exit a conversation is a must. Don't forget the impact of mood memory from chapter 8 of *The 11 Laws of Likability*. You don't want to mar someone's impression of the interaction because of how the conversation ended. After you close the conversation, Susan recommends you "move about one-quarter of the room away. No sense in standing in the same area near the person you just left."

- **Follow Up.** This seems obvious, but often where we leave a conversation is at just that—a single interaction. The goal is to create a connection, to build off the conversation. Think about how to create your next point of contact. Susan's approach is to "devise a system to organize the follow-up process both online and offline." I have a graveyard of business cards on my desk. The truth is, you can't follow up with everyone. Prioritize. My system is if I wrote something on their card, I follow up. Keep it simple and keep the connection going.

Curiosity Is Key

Curiosity is the foundation of being social; it enables connection and Connectors are fundamentally curious people. They like interacting with others because they are inherently intrigued by the world and the people around them. The desire to know more about a person is the fuel for conversation and key to tapping into our social side.

To access your curiosity, don't think, "What should I say?" Instead think, "What should I ask?" Questions drive conversation and the answers lead us to find points of commonality: common interests, values, people, experiences, and causes. The connection is accelerated through the Law of Similarity and associations found in truly listening to the answers.

In a conversation, a Connector balances the use of **advocacy**, stating your view; and **inquiry**, asking questions. When you are advocating, it is your turn to speak and be heard. You are telling a story, sharing a thought, conveying an idea, standing up for something you want or believe in. You are seeking to be understood. Inquiry is seeking to understand the other person's thoughts and ideas. A

Connector with a strength in inquiry will listen beyond the words and ask questions to understand not just what they are saying but the "why" behind the "what."

Inquiry is the foundation for building understanding and creating connection. Effective inquiry will enable you to discover the ways you can add value. Often when a Connector hears what someone is working on, their synapses begin to spark. They are listening to discover what the other person needs, who they want to meet, and how they can be helpful. They are listening to learn, connect, and uncover opportunities to assist. Inquiry helps you figure out the **WIIFT** (what's in it for them) and is one of the keys to persuasion. Whereas advocacy is working toward your **WIIFM** (what's in it for me) and is one of the keys to results.

I always say the best way to get what you want is to figure out why someone else wants you to have it. If you focus on inquiry and leverage your natural curiosity to understand what is important to the other person, then you can advocate for yourself, basing it on accomplishing something that is vital to them. Curiosity sparks a natural desire in us to know or learn something, based on the spirit of inquiry that rests in all of us.

Creative Ways to Connect

Last October I received a notification from LinkedIn that my friend Maria Ross, an Authoress, had mentioned me in a post. I clicked through to a post started by James Carbary, the host of the *B2B Growth* podcast (B2BGrowthShow.com) and a *Huffington Post* contributor. Turns out he was called out for not including more women on his list posts—you know, the posts where you list the top people in a field or experts on a topic.

Stepping up to accept the feedback, he built a list of people creating and distributing original content to follow and asked for suggestions of women to include. (Thanks, Maria!) Being a Connector, I then reached out to James on LinkedIn, which led to a phone call, which led to me asking him to share the unique ways he coaches people to build targeted relationships.

It was the story James told me about creating a scholarship as a way to create relationships with his buyers, who are athletic directors, that grabbed my attention. James started a scholarship competition for their athletes to attend his character-development programs. He sent an email to every athletic director in the state of Texas asking them to nominate two of their student athletes for a $1,000 scholarship. At the end of the campaign, he had contacted every single decision-maker in the state in a value-first way—brilliant! So creative, surprising, and effective.

James poses the question, "What if we are more intentional with the relationships that we create?" I have always talked about being less intentional and to make the friends you want to, rather than the ones you think you should. Perhaps my approach isn't always realistic. So I asked James for some creative ways to be strategic and connect to a target decision-maker or hiring manager or influencer. Here are James's top five creative ways to proactively create relationships with the right people . . . at the right time.

1. **Podcast.** I know this approach isn't for everyone, but podcasting is more accessible than you think. There are companies that can help including James's Sweet Fish Media. His tag line is "Our service allows you to partner with your ideal clients to create industry specific content through an interview-based podcast." As James puts it, "When you ask a potential customer to be a guest on your podcast, there's a good chance they'll say yes. Once someone has been a guest on your show, you have a genuine relationship with them." To prove that genuine relationships actually map to revenue, he shares, "Within an 18-month window of time, our business has done over $165,000 in sales directly from guests that we've featured on our podcast. It just works."

2. Do Free Work. This may not sound enticing, but the truth is, you are probably already doing it. I know I have. The first talk I did for the national organization SIM (Society for Information Management) was unpaid. According to James, "Once you've proven that you do great work, chances are good that they'll end up hiring you." And that's exactly what happened. The head of the organization was in the audience of that free talk and immediately asked me to do the national keynote, paid. From that one free event, I booked four paid talks in the following year. Henry DeVries, CEO of Indie Books International, hosts a free seminar to help consultants learn how to market with a book or speech. I personally know a half-dozen aspiring authors who attended the summit and then hired Henry to help them execute their book projects. As James explains, "If you have a specific skill set, consider offering that skill set at no charge to your dream clients or employers. Build a relationship by making it a no-brainer to work with you."

3. Give a Personalized Gift. James says, "A sure-fire way to create a relationship with someone is through thoughtful gift-giving." This seems obvious, but I admit I could do it more. When I brought a certain CEO a bottle of his favorite tequila, it led to an invitation to meet up again and was the start of a dozen years of mentorship and friendship. James recommends two resources to help. Check out John Ruhlin's book *Giftology* to learn more about the art of strategic gift-giving, and use tools like Alyce.com, which uses personal social data plus your business goals to send the right gifts at the right times to drive action. I suggest sending mail that's bumpy. Sometimes bumpy mail is the first opened. I once sent chocolate to a pregnant producer, which got a great response. When I send a book to someone, I often include my signature pen with the green hair. It always gets a response. According to James, and I agree, "You don't need to spend a lot of money to make an enormous impact."

4. Feature Them. One of the great (and sometimes not-so-great) things about social media is that it gives everyone a voice. As James puts it, "Social media allows each of us to have our own spotlight . . . and we can shine it on anything we want." Instead of posting pictures of your dinner, James suggests you "shine your spotlight on the person that you want to connect with. Talk about the book they wrote, an article they were featured in, or write a 'best of' blog post that includes them at the top of the list." I can attest to the fact that this one works. I have always reached out to connect and thank the author of a list who included me. James calls it "making them look like a rock star." And don't forget to share the link with them when you do.

5. Organize a Group Participation Game. When I was working for a publishing company, one of the C-suite organized the March Madness basketball pool. My officemate was terrified when she called him only to find out it was to tell him he won! She now knew who he was because of it. Whether a pool, a fantasy football league, a book club, or the office lottery ticket, James advises, "Organizing a group can be a great way to create a relationship with someone." Be sure to "invite other people that the person you want to connect with would want to be associated with. So if you're trying to build a relationship with a CEO in the manufacturing industry, invite other manufacturing CEOs, investors, or possible customers to be a part of the group as well."

MINDSET MISSION
Get Curious, Be Social through Questions

Curiosity is an ever-present mindset of the Connector, but it isn't always easy for everyone. Think about the last time you were genuinely curious because you wanted to learn or know more. Rachael O'Meara, author of *Pause: Harnessing the Life-Changing Power of Giving Yourself a Break* (RachaelOMeara.com), shares that when she does this one thing, she instantly relaxes, has more fun, and creates deeper relationships. Her secret? "The next time you find yourself dreading an event or having a mundane conversation, pause and shift your intention to be open and more curious!"

Leveraging the techniques taught in the Law of Curiosity, Rachael provided this Mindset Mission to activate your natural curiosity in your next conversation. Ask yourself these questions:

- What do I want to know or learn about this person right now?
- What question do I really want to know the answer to?
- What can I share (about me, my work, my world) to support this person based on what I'm learning?

Rachael suggests that the ideal social mindset is simply to "drop your agenda or routine, and instead focus on being genuinely curious in the moment. Conversations have a tendency to be more engaging, relaxed, and satisfying." Adopt a **growth mindset**, defined by Carol Dweck, a Stanford University professor, as "a mental attitude that sees challenges as exciting rather than threatening."[1] It makes you more inquisitive. The best part is, each of us is capable of having a growth mindset, but it is a choice we must make deliberately.

REMEMBER, GREAT social interactions do not have to look a certain way. In fact, I met someone who would become one of my best friends, and buddy coach, because we were both speaking at a Columbia University Women in Business event. We arrived at the same time and were trying, unsuccessfully, to get into the building. It was February and snowing, and here was this woman wearing purple suede shoes. I instantly thought that she must be awesome and complimented her shoes. We quickly joked, "How smart do you need to be to make your way into this building?" Every door we tried was locked or required a student ID. By lunchtime that day, it felt like we had known each other for much longer than a few hours. We are still great friends nearly a decade later.

Social happens everywhere. It is about being open, curious, smiling, and having a willingness to share. Social is everything you do, every post you like, and every conversation you have.

Refresh
Your Memory

We are all social beings: introvert, extrovert, or ambivert—it doesn't matter whatsoever when it comes to your ability to connect.

Find your format. Being social can look different for everyone. Select the mode that feels comfortable for you: virtual, group, or one-on-one. Remember to stretch yourself and test out other formats to grow your comfort level and connections.

The introvert's edge. Introverts have innate skills that make them capable Connectors. They are good listeners who know how to make someone feel heard, they focus attention on the person in front of them, and they are best in the one-to-one where true connection forms.

Work the room. If you're going to show up to an event, be positive, enthusiastic, and upbeat—and don't have an agenda. Attend with a friend, or strike up conversations with a lone wolf who would welcome the interaction. Don't forget to follow up to move from conversation to connection.

Leverage your curiosity by balancing advocacy and inquiry. Ask yourself these questions to help conversation flow:

- What do I want to know or learn about this person right now?

- What question do I really want to know the answer to?

- What can I share to support this person based on what I'm learning?

Try creative ways to connect. Think outside the box to connect with a variety of people. Host a podcast, offer to do work gratis, send personalized gifts, or feature them on your social media.

9

Connectors Are Conscientious

"Nothing will work unless you do."

MAYA ANGELOU

You Have to Be Conscious to Be Conscientiousness

Conscientiousness is the personality trait of being careful, or diligent. To be conscientious implies a desire to do a task well and to take obligations to others seriously. You can think of it as personal accountability. According to my survey results, Connectors of all levels are 2.6 times more likely to have positive conscientiousness than Non-Connectors. In other words, if a Connector says they are going to do something, they do it. The follow-up and follow-through lead to credibility and strengthens your positioning in other people's minds as a Connector. The more people see you that way, the more they want to connect with you and the more connected you become. Conscientiousness is an essential part of being a Connector at any level of the spectrum.

Some people are wired for conscientious behavior. They are punctual and organized. They are better at goals: setting them, working toward them, and persisting through setbacks. They are not easily discouraged and always have a plan. We are not all born with those tendencies. For a considerable portion of the population, time is "just a suggestion": they see time as a restrictive and unnecessary boundary. The good news is that, according to the *Journal of Research in Personality*, conscientiousness is a trait that can be cultivated at any point in your life.[1] You become more conscientious by adopting the habits and attitudes of conscientious people.

To be conscientious, you must first be conscious of your current thinking. One thing I found consistent in the research is conscientious people and Connectors have an internal locus of control. My survey revealed an inclination of those self-categorized as Connectors to be 1.7 times more likely to have a strong locus of control. In other words, they believe they are in control of what happens, they take responsibility for themselves and what they do, they do not blame others or the circumstances when something goes wrong. They work hard in the face of challenges and can control their impulses. So the first step in adopting a more conscientious mindset is to begin cultivating the belief that you're in control of your life, and whether you fail or succeed depends on you.

Do What You Say You're Going to Do

Connectors take action. Think about the person in your office or life that you are never sure will follow through with what they promised or the person who you always give an earlier deadline to since you know they will ask for an extension. How do you feel about working with them? A lack of follow-through erodes trust, which damages relationships. If you are one of the many people who needs to work at being conscientious, here are a few suggestions.

Make a Plan

Often the challenge in adopting this mindset is that we try to configure ourselves into how someone else approaches their work or their day. Make your own plan. Consider how you work and when your energy ebbs. I am sharpest in the morning and schedule my thinking activities early, since my brain is much slower later in the day. I track what causes things to fall through the cracks and implement strategies to fill those gaps. I am a huge fan of reminders. That little chime on my phone has saved me from many a missed phone call.

Focus on a specific area of conscientiousness. You are not changing your personality; you are building skills. Simply deciding to be more conscientious will likely not work; it is too vague and broad. Instead, pick a concrete aspect to work on, such as punctuality, scheduling your day, or organizing your office, and craft a SMARTER goal. Part of planning is deciding what to do when things don't work out the way you planned.

Don't Phone It In

Another trait of the conscientious Connector is that they go beyond just doing what they say they will to do it to the best of their ability. There is a difference between doing something and doing it well. A conscientious person takes pride in how they execute a task. They are concerned with doing something correctly. I had an assistant whose work I constantly had to check. There was always a typo, or he didn't send a contract out in time, or he forgot to upload a file: there was always something. He had no attention to detail and didn't seem phased by the constant errors. He didn't last long.

Marshall Goldsmith, bestselling author and renowned leadership coach (MarshallGoldsmith.com), shares an example of conscientiousness from his childhood. "When I was 14, we were very poor and our roof started leaking. My dad hired Dennis Mudd to help us with the roof. They recruited me to help, so we could save a little money. We worked very hard and put on this roof, and you know Dennis is very proud and does the best job he can. When we finished the roof, he looked at my father, Bill, and he said, 'Bill, I want you to inspect the roof. If the roof is high quality, pay me. And if it's not, it's all free.' Dennis Mudd was poor, he needed the money. I looked at

Dennis Mudd and said, 'This man is poor, but he's not cheap. Dennis Mudd has class.'"

Dennis Mudd had more than class; he exemplified conscientiousness. He stood behind his work. To access conscientious behaviors, double-check your work. Ask questions to ensure you are clear on the task and the desired outcomes. When you deliver, explain how the product ties back to the definition of success for the project. If you, like me, can't see the typos, find a work buddy to proof it for you and do the same for them. Often those details are hard to catch when you can only see what you expect to see. If you want to encourage this approach, give and ask for feedback. Pride in your work is reinforced when you receive recognition for it.

Follow Up

Things fall off the radar. It happens to the most conscientious of us. Think about how you process your to-do list. What happens when something moves to someone else's list before it comes back to you? That is often where things get lost in the shuffle. For example, when you check in with a client, or pass a request along, you can cross the task off your list. What happens if they don't respond? Do you remember to check in again? It feels great to cross off a task, but there are often more stages in a task then done or not done. I have a WIP folder for work in progress that I review weekly. You can find your own way to catch those things that don't require immediate action but are not truly completed.

I am often asked how to determine the balance between thorough follow-up with a new contact and pestering. When is waiting too long, too late? I refer to the rule of threes. I don't think one reach-out without a response should end the attempt to build a connection. I do recommend extending the time between each reach-out. After three attempts across a few months, I would not persist. I may put them on a list for a six-month follow-up and see if it was just bad timing. A possible subject line is "This fell off our radar." No response after that and I move on. As for too late, timely is ideal, but in the Connector's mind a potential connection is never too late. I have had business cards sitting for six months collecting dust and will still send an email. The subject line may be, "Just found your card" or "It's been a while," so that the follow-up is immediately personalized.

Close the Loop

Part of doing what you say you are going to do is not just the execution but the follow-through of circling back and closing the loop. It's similar to following up your answer to a question by asking, "Does that answer your question?" Closing the loop takes it beyond your part in the process and considers the bigger picture, the reason you were performing that task. You can close the loop by checking with a teammate that they have everything they need or inquiring about the progress of the project even if your part is long completed.

Closing the loop is critical to Connectors who are reaping the benefit and assistance of their connections. Let's say Devyn made an introduction for you. Let her know you followed through on her outreach. It is respecting what someone else has done for you. You are not just representing yourself, you are representing whoever made that initial introduction for you. You don't have to copy them on every email exchange. I typically move the Connector to a bcc, so they know we have connected while saving their inbox from excess emails. To truly close the loop, I will circle back with Devyn and let her know the outcome of the conversation and her effort.

I will often mention Devyn with my new connection, reinforcing that she made the connection, adding value for her and also building trust with the connection. Always let someone know what their efforts resulted in. Don't make them wonder! Prove that they were right to do whatever they did for you. Give the credit and appreciation as you close the loop. After my first book came out, I sent copies with personal inscriptions to all the people who helped me. Closing the loop is about not forgetting the people who helped you get there, no matter how long ago that help might have been. Regardless of whether or not their efforts created results, appreciate the effort more than the result.

Four Communication Hacks

I was invited to be on the *World of Speakers* podcast hosted by three-time TEDx speaker and communication guru Ryan Foland (RyanFoland.com). As I always try to do, I chatted with Ryan before and after the show. That conversation sparked this sidebar with his simple hacks for meeting new people and networking events.

- **Be Easy to Read.** When it comes to meeting people you've never met before, first impressions really *are* critical. Ryan asked me, "Did you know that your face makes over 4,000 micro movements that other people can pick up on subconsciously?" I didn't! According to Ryan, these tiny alterations in your facial expressions communicate volumes to people, whether you realize it or not. Humans are trained to constantly evaluate situations to make sure you are in a safe environment. Ryan and I agree that the best way to let people know you are not a threat is simple—smile! People who smile are approachable, people who don't are not. When you scan a room, your subconscious picks up signals from faces in the crowd. You are more likely to connect with those who look like they're in a good mood, return eye contact, and give you signals that they are open to a conversation. Smile in the middle of conversation to acknowledge a point made, smile just to smile, and you will find others smiling back at you. This low-tech tip is one of the most powerful that you can use and it extends well beyond networking. Try to smile more in your regular day-to-day interactions and you will invite conversations, connections, and opportunities that you may have missed.

- **Get Them Talking.** One of the best tactics in a networking situation is active listening and ensuring you are listening out and not just listening in as explained in chapter 6 of *The 11 Laws of Likability*. The fact is, people like to talk. Ryan shares, "There are studies that show a correlation between the amount of time that someone talks and how connected they feel with a conversation." Therefore, Ryan advises, "If you want to build quicker relationships with people you've just met, get them to talk *more*." To do this, Ryan wants you to "pay attention and understand what they're saying so you can ask better questions based on the information they're providing." When you focus on listening, you will be more engaged in the conversation, create positive mood memory for the person talking, and increase the likelihood that you will have a second conversation. Learn to listen, and listen to learn about the other person.

- **Know How to Communicate the Problem You Solve.** When Ryan consults with leaders on creating more buy-in for their products and services, he teaches them to start with the problem they solve. You already know from chapter 5 that people are driven by WIIFT. You will be a more compelling contact if you can solve a problem. When someone asks you what you do, "phrase your answer in a way that communicates the problem you solve, without telling them what you do." When you do, you will notice that people who are interested in the problem will ask you more information. I thought it was an interesting approach; instead of saying, "I am a trainer or coach," I could say, "I help people work better together." When Ryan employs this hack, it leads into a natural conversation about what he does to solve that problem. As he puts it, "By slightly changing the order of information offered, you will not only catch their attention, but create intrigue and keep the conversation going."

- **Create a Memory Flash.** The advice *be memorable* is easier said than done. At a networking event, you may meet dozens of people; it's hard to remember everyone. So how do you stand out? Ryan explains that you want to "create an anchor memory in their brain." His way of doing this is right before the conversation ends, Ryan "will ask them to come up with a code word. People typically are confused. I ask them to come up with a word that makes them remember our interaction or conversation; anything that comes to the top of their mind at that moment such as something we talked about or the event itself." He then puts the code word in the subject line of his follow-up email. "That word created a mental anchor in their brain." The funny thing is, this happened to me unintentionally with Kristen Pressner and the word "Blerg!" See chapter 11 for the full story.

Know When to Say *No* and How to Say *Yes*

Let me be clear: conscientious doesn't mean saying yes to everything. Connectors say no; they just know how and when to say no. The fact is, it's hard to say no. You don't want to give an answer someone doesn't want to hear. It's uncomfortable. You feel rude, think your peers will find you unhelpful, or worry that your boss will think you are not dedicated. Sometimes you want to say yes but then overextend yourself and need to remember no is an option. My husband taped the word *no* to my monitor for a year to remind me that I needed to say it more often. He was right. To be conscientious, and do what you say you are going to do, you must be selective about what you commit to. You need to know when and how to say no. When saying no is not an option, you must also learn how to say yes.

Recently a loose family relation, whom I'm not close with, emailed me and asked me to speak at a midweek dinner for her local professional group. The event was an hour away from my home, the drive would be during rush hour and my family time, they didn't have a budget, and the audience size was a few dozen people. If it hadn't been a relative, saying no would have been easy. I used a response technique I call **No, But**. I shared my pro bono policy and requirements and said, "I am not able to say yes to this event, *but* if you join with another group and are able to meet the minimum participation or… please reach back out." I gave her multiple ways to get a yes in the future and explained my reasons for saying no to the request. It was still hard, but it was the right answer for me.

The response technique you choose is based on the priority of the request and the relationship you have with the person making the ask. Table 9.1 shows the response options for those spectrums and a suggested response technique.

Table 9.1: When to Say No and How to Say Yes

PRIORITY	RELATIONSHIP	CHOICE	TECHNIQUE
Low	Low	Decline or Question	No Yes, If Yes, When Yes, After
Low to moderate	Moderate	Redefine	Qualified No No with Alternatives Yes with Alternatives
Low to moderate	High	Reprioritize	No, But Yes, If Yes with Alternatives
High	High	Accept	Yes

When the relationship and request are both low, saying no is much easier. So simply say no, or "no, thank you" if it feels better to you. Avoid saying, "I am sorry, no." First, you have nothing to be sorry for; you are allowed to say no. Second, it leaves the door open to them not accepting the no and pushing you toward a yes you really don't want to give. If your position or relationship requires your answer to be yes, a no can be framed as **Yes, If**. First, question more about the request such as, "Is it higher priority than…?" or "Are you open to another person assisting you?" or "Would _____ be an option?" With more information you can answer, "Yes, if it is urgent" or "Yes, if no one else is available." This enables the person asking to reevaluate *if* it is something they really need *you* to do.

As the relationship increases in importance, the yes or no response will soften. You can redefine the ask with a **Qualified No**. "I can't do it all, but I can help you with..." or "I am not available now, but can find time on..." You can also mutually reprioritize by saying either "No, but I can do it after I finish" or "I am not able to help, but I can suggest a few people that may be interested." The Qualified No can be turned into a qualified yes or a **Yes with Alternatives**. Try, "Yes, I can help you get that done; which task do you want to tackle first?" or "Yes, I can help you identify some resources to do that."

Personally, I am a huge fan of the alternatives option and rely on it often. I can only take on a limited number of coaching clients. When my son's teacher asked me to speak to her husband who was starting a business, I was happy to. When he wanted to hire me as a coach, I used the alternatives approach by providing information about more cost-effective group coaching options. I forwarded him resources to assist but was firm with my no. This tactic enables you to still feel comfortable and good in the relationship and does not risk the long-term connection.

Saying yes is easy. What makes a yes the right answer is ensuring it is aligned with your capacity and priorities. If you decide to say yes, consider that there are many ways to say yes: **Yes, If; Yes, After; Yes, When**. Any time your capacity or skill inhibits your ability to accomplish the task, the right answer is "Yes, with help": "I would be happy to do that but need help reassigning these tasks"; "Yes, I can do that if there is training offered." Say yes and make sure it is a yes you can actually do and do well.

WHEN I think of this mindset, the word "trustworthy" always comes up. But trustworthy isn't a mindset—it's something that's earned. It's a perception that others have of you that can only be attained by being conscientious *over time*. Conscientiousness has many definitions, but the one I like the best is simply: "follow through." When a person is thoughtful about the choices they make and is clear about what they are willing to say yes and no to, when they do what they say they're going to do, and when they execute tasks with full effort, eventually they develop a reputation that they're a trustworthy person. It is among the Connector's most important traits.

Refresh
Your Memory

Conscientiousness is a key trait in Connectors, who are 2.6 times more likely to have positive conscientiousness than Non-Connectors. If a Connector says they are going to do something, they do it.

Do what you say you are going to do. Conscientiousness can be cultivated. You are not changing your personality; you are building skills.

Make a plan. Deciding to be more conscientious is too vague and broad. Instead, pick a concrete aspect to work on such as punctuality, scheduling your day, or organizing your office. Part of planning is figuring out what to do when things don't work out the way you planned.

Don't phone it in. Do everything to the best of your ability. There is a difference between doing something and doing it well. A conscientious person takes pride in how they execute a task.

Follow up and follow through. Part of doing what you say you are going to do is not just the execution but the follow-through of circling back and closing the loop. Follow-up and follow-through leads to credibility and strengthens your position in other people's minds as a Connector.

Try a communication hack. Make a good first impression, be an active listener, and ask follow-up questions in a conversation. When you're telling other people about your work, start by explaining the problem you solve.

Know how to say yes and no. A Connector is conscientious about what they commit to, and they don't say yes to every request. There are multiple ways to say yes such as **Yes, If; Yes, After;** and **Yes, When.** Saying no is easier when you provide alternatives. Try **No, But** or a **Qualified No.**

10

Connectors Have a Generous Spirit

"We make a living by what we get,
but we make a life by what we give."

WINSTON CHURCHILL

Generosity Is Exponential

I am passionate about this mindset. It is intrinsically linked with the tenth law of likability, the Law of Giving. I am often expounding the ideals of give first, give often, give because you can, and give without the expectation of getting anything in return. Generosity inherently creates value—that value can be hard to track, but it's infectious!

Someone with a generous spirit exhibits a readiness to give more of something than is strictly necessary or expected. It is an approach to life and does not depend on your circumstances. A homeless man was given $100 and bought food and distributed it to others in need. That YouTube video, "How Does a Homeless Man Spend $100?" has always stuck with me.[1]

A generous spirit is one that engages others with an open heart and mind, without judgment, and is accepting of different beliefs, values, and behaviors. A person with a generous spirit assumes positive intent, embraces difference, and is genuinely happy for others' good fortune. They are not without jealousy, but that momentary twinge does not drive their words or actions.

I read this description and it seems out of reach; I think to myself, "Do I truly adopt a generous spirit?" I make these people sound like saints; they are not. It takes conscious effort to choose a generous mindset. To embrace it requires you to expend energy on looking for what is good or admirable about a person or situation, to look for the opportunities to add value, to question your assumptions and conclusions. That is all within reach.

There are many ways to act on your generous spirit, but it is the spirit itself that exemplifies a Connector. I saw this mindset so clearly during my conversation with acclaimed leadership coach Marshall Goldsmith. He epitomizes a generous spirit: "I don't have any intellectual property, I give away everything. Anybody can use any of my stuff any way they want to. All you do is you go online. Read whatever you want to read—use it, copy it, download, share with anybody you want to, put your name on it. I don't care." Marshall has recently "adopted" 100 coaches to whom he will teach his wealth of knowledge. His only payment: that they pay it forward in some way.

Marshall shares a story from his youth that illustrates this approach to people and life. When he was stationed in Kentucky, he was in charge of the March of Dimes bread drive. The way it was supposed to work was "you knock on the door and ask for a donation. When someone gives you a donation, you give them a loaf of bread. They do not give you a donation, you don't give them a loaf of bread." Marshall told his team, "We're going to do this differently. When people open the door, you give them a loaf of bread. If they want to donate something, fine. If they don't want to donate, you give them a loaf of bread anyway!" His approach was if they're too poor to give you any money, just give them the bread. His team was in the poorest neighborhood, so they probably should've come in near last place in terms of collection. "We won by 20%," he shares with pride.

His theory is that "most people are nice people and if you're generous with them and nice, then they'll be generous and nice to you too! That's just the way people are." That thinking enables him to embody the spirit of generosity.

There Is Always Value to Add

The key to having a generous spirit is being genuinely *happy* about giving. It goes hand in hand with the abundant mindset: not only do you have enough, but when you share—be it time, contacts, knowledge, or resources—you feel good about it. You're not resentful or regretful and you don't keep a scorecard waiting for when you will be "paid" back.

Sometimes it can be hard to realize just how much you have to give. I hear this often when people are seeking mentors or building a connection with someone further along in their career or the hierarchy. I get it. I have felt that many times and still do. You want to build relationships with both the more and less experienced. Over the last dozen years, I have grown a relationship with a highly successful CEO, who I was introduced to by a mutual friend. Even though he knocked down my business idea in the first 10 minutes we spoke, that didn't prevent or discourage the relationship from continuing. I have tried to be helpful to him over the years, but in all honesty it has been minimal in comparison. Note to self: people with a generous spirit are not keeping a scorecard!

A couple of years ago at a bar, I said, "You know, you're a mentor to me." He smiled and laughed. In my mind, he's more valuable to me than I am to him. But that doesn't mean I haven't been able to add value; there is always value to add. I have made introductions. Once I was able to get him a specific superhero T-shirt he wanted from Target; at the time, there were none near his home in the heart of New York City. Recently, I told him about a home remedy for healing a sty. Perhaps him knowing how much his advice has helped me is in itself valuable to him.

Even though you may not necessarily feel like you are at the person's level professionally, you still have plenty to give. Having a generous spirit does not mean you have to make grand gestures. My editor on this book once worked for a high-power media executive whose iPhone was always getting buried at the bottom of her purse. She showed her how to make it flash when it's ringing, a feature invented for the deaf and hearing impaired. Her executive was thrilled. It is often the little things that mean the most. A heartfelt thank-you for a job well done or an act of kindness—making someone feel extra-appreciated is in itself a gift. Here are some ideas for Connectors to infuse value in generous acts.

How to Make an Introduction

One of the most common acts of a Connector is simply to connect other people. It is the fundamental way Connectors apply their generous spirit. Sounds simple, but making an introduction like a Connector is nuanced. Before offering the introduction, Connectors consider what's in it for both parties. There is a reason a Connector thought to connect two people and they share that reason.

In the communication, explain to both sides why they'd be interested, indicating the potential value for both sides. Sometimes the value isn't clear, yet I think two people should meet. If you have that situation, make the introduction. Simply state, "I don't know exactly what you guys will talk about it, but I think you might really like to connect." As a Connector, people trust your connections, you have credibility. Someone seeking to embrace a Connector mindset will be open to meeting someone new without knowing exactly why. In addition to the reason why to connect, include information about each person in the introduction. I may include how I know them, a link to their online profile or website, or a topic to kick off the conversation. The goal is to make it easy for the two parties to get a sense of one another right away.

Certain situations require a tweak to the introduction process. For example, when the people are not necessarily going to receive similar value from the connection. When my friend introduced me to my future mentor, the CEO, she asked his permission first. That was exactly the right approach. You don't want to make an introduction that puts someone in the position of *having* to respond because of their relationship with you. Connectors do favors for Connectors because that's how they roll. Be honest about why you are making the intro and manage their expectations for results. Don't oversell it; if they are doing you a favor, let them know you view it that way too. Second, you don't want to extend your reputation to someone who you don't know well enough. Make the introduction, but be clear on the level of connection you have with them.

Sometimes both aspects exist. Recently I met another author, Priya, who was producing a conference and looking for speakers. Immediately, I thought of Holly, a Broadway producer who I thought would be ideal for the conference. I wasn't sure if Holly would be interested: she is not a professional speaker, and I didn't know Priya well. I asked Priya to send me more info about it and then forwarded it to Holly asking if she was interested. She was, and I put them in touch. If they don't circle back, I'll reach out and ask if anything came of it. Even if they don't close the loop, you can. It's an excuse to follow up and further build those connections.

How to Amplify Impact

A generous spirit seeks to amplify the impact of the great things others are doing. Amplification can be through sharing their message on social media, by retelling the story of their efforts, by enlisting others to join their cause, or by paying their generosity forward to someone else. I first told you about Amy in chapter 10 of *The 11 Laws of Likability*. When I was a wannabe entrepreneur, Amy, an established woman in business, was so generous with her time and advice. She actually gave me the courage to, as she put it, "hang out my shingle and say 'open for business!'" Although eventually, I was able to reciprocate some of the value she created for me, there were many years when I couldn't. Instead, I amplified her generosity by paying it forward and giving my time to up-and-coming entrepreneurs.

I was telling this story during a speech at a local university and said, "I've now sat with over 100 people." Someone in the audience called out, "I'm one of them!" I squinted to see who it was, smiled, and waved at Donovan. Then I heard a woman's voice near him say, "Me too!" It became a cacophony throughout the room with about half the hands going up and saying, "Me too!" I was in tears and could only think to say, "I guess I need to change my number!" My best guess now is that I've probably spoken with more than 500 people as they started their business, and the number grows. That's what I mean by exponential impact. Amy had no idea how her generosity of spirit would inevitably impact so many people, but it did.

In 2015, I created a positive sharing campaign with my kids by posting a "#365LivingGiving" video on YouTube.[2] My goal was to amplify more messages about acts of kindness and the good in the world. I wanted my kids to hear a more balanced message than the horrors of the daily news. Darrah Brustein, founder of Network Under 40 (Darrah.co), started the #GiveItForward challenge, offering to help one person a day to get closer to their goals, dreams, or needs with no strings attached. I loved her passionate plea: "No matter how much money is in your bank account or how much free time you have, we all have the capacity to help someone else. And in that process, we inevitably become happier and more successful ourselves." Within 24 hours, more than 300 people from all over the world joined in and began to share the beautiful stories of what unfolded when they asked the simple question, "How can I help you today?"

Amplification is about the other person and can simply be highlighting the impact someone's work, words, or actions had on those around them. Who or what do you want to amplify?

How to Add Value at the Office

In the corporate world, being generous often means trying to add value to another's work, even before they ask you. Generosity is a mindset of initiating, and it's even more important as you rise up the ladder, because you have more ability and value to give. In the work environment, generosity is sometimes feared. You may worry if you give credit to others, your accomplishments will be minimized. Maybe you fear that you will be taken advantage of. I am not so naive as to think those things couldn't happen; there are risks. If you have clarity on your goals and are conscientious about what you say yes to, you minimize those risks. Relationships will get you further than fear.

I told you about my husband Michael's evolution to Acting Connector in chapter 3. When he was at the Responsive Connector level, waiting for people to ask for something, I questioned, "Why make them ask? Asking is hard. Can you come up with an idea and then offer it? You have so much to give." Information, invitations, introductions, admiration, advice, appreciation, recognition, credit, and a simple thanks are all accessible ways to add value. Everyone has a desire to give back; it's about going from desire to action and recognizing you have value to add.

It doesn't matter where you are in the hierarchy of life—you may think you're paying it forward, but that person you helped may leapfrog you and pull you up along with them. With a generous philosophy, we all climb.

Set Boundaries

Adopting a generous mindset can be tricky. There is a balance between being giving and being taken advantage of, or giving to the detriment of yourself or loved ones. When Marshall Goldsmith gives away his coaching processes and resources for free, he exudes the mindset of the generous spirit and comes from a place of total abundance. Marshall can do that at this point in his life. That is not realistic or wise for everyone. You don't have to give away the farm to embrace a generous spirit. Boundaries are necessary to enable you to maintain the mindset. Refer back to the last chapter and get comfortable with how to say yes and when to say no.

The truth is, it is possible to be *too* generous, a trap that catches women more often than men. Elisa Camahort Page, cofounder of BlogHer, and author of *Road Map for Revolutionaries: Resistance, Activism, and Advocacy for All* (ElisaCP.com), points out that there is a difference between having a generous spirit and being a doormat, and the difference is the boundaries you set. You can learn more about and from Elisa in the sidebar. She and I have faced some similar struggles balancing our desire to give with giving until it hurts. It happens in all industries: the doctor who is asked to "take a quick look" while at a dinner party; the accountant's answer about a tax loophole; the financial advisor's favorite stock; the recruiter who gets résumés from every friend of a friend for feedback; the real estate agent's opinion on your home's value.

When you are in a career where your product is your expertise, it is sometimes hard to differentiate for the person asking and for you to set boundaries. I don't want to discourage people from asking; rather, I want to encourage you to determine your limits. Remember the definition of a generous spirit is to not feel resentful of the act of giving; when you do, perhaps that is an indication of where you need to set your boundary.

This mindset comes with pitfalls which is why boundaries are important. Keep in mind these possible drawbacks when adopting a generous mindset.

Giving Something Unwanted. Sometimes a Connector is so eager to help, they may help in a way that is unhelpful. As you have likely experienced in your relationships, sometimes a person just wants to be listened to and understood. They don't want you to "fix it" for them. Ask them if they want an ear or an assist; get direction from them on their needs in the moment. If it is information or an introduction, check their interest in it before you act. When you give something unwanted, you may make the person feel obligated or annoyed and put the relationship at risk.

Spreading Yourself Too Thin. There is advice throughout the book on how to manage time, when to say no, and how to say yes. Don't deplete yourself along the way. A competent Connector knows when they need to pull back.

Being Taken Advantage Of. Others can often see this better than the Connector in the moment. Not everyone has the shared mindset and approach. People can take advantage of your generosity. Decide what you will be comfortable with giving regardless of the permanence of the relationship.

Something for Nothing Is Never Really Nothing

I asked Elisa to explain the difference between having a generous spirit and being burdened by inappropriate asks. She shares, "I've seen the cycle many times. Someone new to an industry, business, or career leaps at any opportunity, including opportunities that leverage their skills, but pay badly, or even pay only in 'exposure' or an 'expanded network' or some other non–revenue-generating value. At some point, exposure and networking are not enough ROI and mantras about 'Know your worth' and 'I can't pay my rent with exposure' fill your head."

We both believe in owning your expertise, knowing its value, and asking for what you deserve. At the same time, Elisa believes, "Operating with a generous spirit, believing in giving back and the possibility of abundance, and knowing when to give without expectation of immediate return is in the toolkit of every exceptional leader." So how do you make the call?

For me, I created a decision tree to test the situation against a set of criteria. I also created a limit to the number of events in a given timeframe. It helped me be more objective about requests rather than acting on my desire to give every time. Elisa articulates her boundaries when responding to requests to leverage her expertise by saying, "I consult on this very topic, but I am always happy to spend an hour with any friend or friend of a friend gratis . . . Let's set up a call."

In our conversation, it was clear that Elisa champions one of the main tenets of relationship networking: it's not about me. Her definition of the purpose of networking is "to connect two or more parties for their mutual benefit, with the understanding that you may not be one of the parties, and the benefit may not occur now." Elisa doesn't approach generosity as a transaction. She embraces that the return doesn't always have to be for her. She recognizes that "not every person I can help will always be able to help me, perhaps ever." But she is firm in her knowledge that being known as someone who builds, sustains, and supports productive relationships will always help her. In the end, Elisa decides when to donate her time and energy. She puts it perfectly: "Only I can decide if it's worth it." Doing something for nothing is never really for nothing.

Be Generous with Yourself

A generous spirit is not about putting others before yourself. You need to be generous with yourself as well. You know the things you need to do take good care of *you*, whether it's time on the treadmill or even a nap before a big meeting. People who are great at this mindset actually slot the time in their calendar to do them (even if it means asking others to pick up a little slack). I never took care of myself—no gym, no relaxation, nothing—until only a few years ago, and then I realized I needed to make those things fit into my crazy schedule. Boundaries helped and enabled me to reprioritize. That meant I may have spoken with a few less people or had people wait longer to connect, and I had to remind myself that was okay.

I have to acknowledge the constant internal battle that many mothers and some fathers face: the choice between staying at home with the kids and working. No matter which you've chosen, you will feel like there's something missing, or that there is an external judgment of your choice. What I came to realize as a working mom is that I feel happier and more fulfilled having a professional purpose. I'm a good mom, even though I'm not president of the PTA. Being generous with yourself is about knowing your own needs and not feeling guilty about them.

If you have a Connector mindset, and become aware that someone needs something or someone requests something of you, your inclination is to figure out how to help. Remember sometimes you have to help yourself and just say no.

WHEN I am talking with someone, I am listening and learning about them. I'm making connections in my brain—finding points of similarity, associations, and common interests. I am listening to learn about them and looking for ways to add value. A Connector gets pleasure from being able to do that. It's not purely altruistic: there is something in it for the Connector, that something is often intangible satisfaction or goodwill. Connectors know that what they do and give comes back to them and their community. This enables them to make requests and get results without an expectation of immediate reciprocity. With boundaries, anyone can adopt a generous spirit.

Refresh
Your Memory

Adopt a generous spirit. Engage with others with an open heart and without judgment. Be tolerant of different beliefs, values, and behaviors. Assume positive intent and embrace differences with acceptance. Be happy for others' good fortune. Don't allow understandable moments of jealousy to drive your words or actions.

Add value. You have plenty to give and can help in a multitude of ways. You do not have to make grand gestures. Information, invitations, introductions, admiration, advice, appreciation, recognition, credit or a simple thanks are all accessible ways to add value.

Amplify the impact of the great things others are doing. Give credit, share their story, enlist others, or simply pay it forward.

Set boundaries. There is a balance between being giving and being taken advantage of, or giving to the detriment of yourself or your loved ones. Remember, sometimes you have to help yourself and just say no.

Be generous with yourself. You know the things you need to do to take good care of *you*. Slot the time into your calendar to do them.

Diversify: Expand the Way You Connect

The most successful people are often the most connected. Part of being connected is building a network that crosses interests, industry, hierarchy, ethnicity, age, geography, and more. Diverse teams and organizations make better decisions. Diverse networks give you access to different viewpoints, access to information, and extended connections. In this section, I delve into how to expand the way you connect from the types of people you connect with to the communication channels and technology tools you use.

11

LinkedIn and Technology Tools

"'Build it, and they will come' only works in the movies. Social media is a 'build it, nurture it, engage them, and they may come and stay.'"

SETH GODIN

I ADMIT IT: technology is not my thing. I would be lost without it, but it is still not my thing. There seem to be more tools invented daily to help us be visible, stay connected, share, post, update, tweet, pin, and check in. There are dozens, if not hundreds, of social media platforms. There are definitely dos and don'ts of the digital world to be aware of. This chapter addresses the platforms, some of those dos and don'ts, and other technology tools to help diversify the way we connect.

Every social site has its own personality and how you engage, who you connect to, and what you post are driven by the site's personality. One of the first I ever used, and still believe in today, is LinkedIn. It is the manifestation of everything I say, teach, and write. In fact, their mission statement is very similar to my own in writing this book: "The mission of LinkedIn is simple: connect the world's professionals to make them more productive and successful." LinkedIn is an amazing tool for seeing how you are linked to different people through other connections, organizations, geographies, interest groups, and more. The key to using it effectively is to strengthen and increase those links both on and offline.

To Link or Not to Link

If you're on LinkedIn, I'm guessing you get lots of requests from people you don't know. I know I do. If you're wondering whether or not you should accept those requests, you're not alone. My old philosophy was I would only accept the request if you met one of three criteria: 1) I knew you already; 2) I could figure out why you were reaching out—perhaps we went to the same school, worked at the same company, or are in the same industry; or 3) you sent a personal note explaining why you wanted to connect. Otherwise, I would ignore the request. For most people, this approach works and makes people comfortable. The result is a network that you know and feel comfortable reaching out to and that you're able to assist.

My philosophy now is a little different, because my profession is about reach and I want my content to touch more people. I now accept most, though still not all, of the requests I get. I'll happily accept requests from anyone who has heard me speak, listened to me on a podcast, bought my book... you get the idea. All it takes is a note that tells me the reason they want to connect. The likelihood is that they will get a personalized email and LinkedIn message back from me. If you haven't written me with a note explaining why you want to connect, I often still accept if the profile looks legitimate (and not a potential spammer). I then send a note asking how they found me or what made them reach out. It surprises me how many people do not respond. One who did was Kristen Pressner and look how that turned out! She is not only in chapter 6 but also contributed a Mindset Mission in chapter 12. We connected because she reached out to me blindly on LinkedIn. I'll never forget her response to my asking her how she found me. She said, "Blerg! For the life of me I can't recall!" and I laughed out loud. I emailed back, "Blerg is the *best* word!" We've since Skyped multiple times and she graciously agreed to be included and share her expertise in this book! All because I grew a relationship with her personally, beyond LinkedIn.

If you are going to link, don't mistake an accepted connection as a real connection. To create that, more has to happen after you link. Look at their profile. I always glance at shared connections, scroll through their experience and education to see if we have overlaps. I love the interests section for the unexpected common causes. Send a message through the platform or pull their email address from contact info and send them a direct email. Not everyone checks their LI messages regularly. If you think you have nothing to say, try asking how they know one of your shared connections or how they like working for their current company. Sometimes just a simple note saying "Thanks for reaching out" is enough to show you are willing to expand the relationship. However you respond, don't just click "accept." Offer a conversation.

One reason to accept more invitations than you reject is to see the exponential impact to your network and how you show up in searches or on other people's suggested connections. Be aware that social media is rife with fake accounts, and LinkedIn is not immune. If you are unsure, wait a few days. Fake accounts are often removed quickly. When you're deciding whether or not to link with someone, consider what your goals are in your life and work. When you connect on LinkedIn, you're opening the door for that person to make requests of you, and you to make requests of them. Plenty of users put the word LION next to their names to signify that they are LinkedIn Open Networkers, ready and willing to connect with the multitudes. If you are reaching out, look for opportunities to expand the connection either virtually or offline. The point is to make a real connection, not just rack up the numbers.

How to Reach Out on LinkedIn

Reaching out on LinkedIn should happen in both directions. When I first created a profile, I spent a few minutes every week thinking of people I knew and reaching out to them. Then I thought about the companies I had worked for and the schools I had attended and continued to send LinkedIn invitations. One way to expand your network is to reignite the network that may have faded over time and to extend your personal network to a professional platform.

If you already know the person, it is easy to reach out. I would still recommend including a personal note. Our memories fade over time. Make it easy for them to accept by reminding them how you know each other. Reaching out when you haven't met offline takes a little more nuance. You have a choice between following someone and connecting with them. Ask yourself why are you reaching out to this person. If it is someone you admire, someone of high stature in your field, or someone you are interested in learning about, but not necessarily forming a personal connection with, you may want to consider following them instead of sending an invitation to connect.

Following a person ensures their updates show up in your feed. You receive their articles and posts in your notifications. It does not make you first connections and you do not need their permission to follow them; it is a one-way relationship. You are consuming their public content and keeping up on changes in their profile. If your goal is to build a relationship, invite them to connect. If they accept your invitation, it creates a two-way relationship where they also see your posts and you can send them unlimited-character direct messages. Following someone first can make the invitation to connect later easier.

If the reason you are reaching out is because of someone or something you have in common, requesting a connection is easier. In the invitation, tell the person what inspired you to reach out. Below are some common reasons and potential introductory statements to use when reaching out to someone you don't know.

Shared Connection: Most of the time using the name of a shared connection builds immediate trust, assuming they actually know the person. Typically, if you know the shared contact well, you do not need to seek permission to mention their name. The caveat is if you are putting any words in their mouth such as, "Maria suggested I reach out" or "Diego thought we should connect." In those scenarios, seek permission first. Other options include:

- "Your name popped up on people I might know. Have we met?" or "... Would you like to connect?"
- "I see that you know ____. How do you two know each other? I actually grew up with her. Such a small world."
- "It looks like we have tons of people in common. I am surprised our paths have not crossed sooner. Let's connect."

Shared Industry or Organization: Reaching out for obvious professional reasons is often the most easily accepted invite, especially if you are already employed. I strongly recommend building your industry network before you need it for the job search. If you are considering a move to a new industry, you can use that in your invitation. People will be most hesitant to connect if you are clearly trying to sell something. Consider reaching out with an offer and not an ask. Try:

- "I see that we're both in the _____ field. I am considering a move and am interested in learning more about your firm. How do you like the organization?"
- "I see we both belong to the same group. Would you like to connect?" or "Do you find it valuable?" or "What do you hope to get out of it?" or "Are you interested in other groups? There are a few I find beneficial."
- "I saw you work for _____. I used to work there. Let's connect." or "Does _____ still work there?" or "I am interested in learning more about the company. Are you open to connecting?"

Shared Interest: A shared interest is a looser professional link, but often a stronger personal one. The invite recipient rarely feels skeptical of the reach-out with a nonprofessional personalized reason. If you do follow the same person or organization, share how or why you got involved. For example:

- "I see you also follow _____. I find the _____ content particularly valuable. What made you follow them?"
- "I see you support _____. Have you heard of any opportunities to get more involved lately?"
- "We are both members of _____. I am looking for additional groups. Are there any you find worthwhile?"

Seeking to add value to your potential new contact is always a great approach. Phrases like "mutually beneficial" or "possibility to collaborate" or "help each other" are fine if realistic. If you are fresh out of school and reaching out to a CEO, it is not appropriate to tell them it is in their interest to connect with you. Are you connecting as a peer or for advice? If you are reaching out to someone at a higher professional level, be honest and simply say you are "seeking advice" or "you have a quick question" and you will be more likely to hear back.

A connection request that will not work is this one I actually received: "I would like to try LinkedIn to find new customers. I decided to give it a go and I would like to follow up with content and posting. I hope this works." Needless to say, I did not accept the request. Another faux pas came from someone whose request I did accept. There was no note, but I accepted and then emailed asking what made him reach out. His response was: "Hello Michelle, I recently downloaded the LinkedIn application for my phone. It then asked for all the emails in my phone and it sent out 3,000 emails asking folks like you to connect." He went on to acknowledge it was a mistake and we had a humorous exchange. It ended up working for him, but I would be wary of sending a mass connection request. I am betting many people ignored his generic reach-out.

Whatever approach you try, a personalized note will always increase your odds of a positive response. You may not get a response at all. Don't take it personally. Many people are busy and not as active on LinkedIn as you might be. I have received responses months after reaching out.

How to Engage on LinkedIn

LinkedIn is a relationship platform. Just as first impressions matter in person, they also matter online. First things first, create a complete profile; fill out all sections robustly. Add your skills, put in details and lots of keywords to increase your searchability. A photo is an absolute must! Don't give me excuses. There is a direct correlation between the likelihood of someone connecting and you having a photo. That picture increases trust. It should be a professional-looking head-and-shoulders shot but does not need to be taken by a professional. No photos that clearly crop out another person and, unless you are a cartoonist, no cartoon images. Check out the sidebar for more tips on optimizing your profile.

Once your profile is ready, and you are growing your connections, the next step is to engage on the platform. People use it to search for jobs and job candidates, consume content, share expertise and resources, join community groups, and more. There is an etiquette to engaging on any social media platform. How you engage is based on your goals. One goal is simply to increase your familiarity and name recognition by having a presence online. Below are some methods for engaging and some things to avoid doing on LinkedIn.

Updates, Posts, and Comments

This is the easiest way to engage on LinkedIn. You can post a status update on your page, which will be shared with your network based on your privacy settings. It will also appear in your activity if someone views your profile. Posts can be text only, text with an image, an article, or a video. Posts have a lower word-count limit than articles and they are stored differently in your activity archive. An easy way to engage is simply to like or share someone else's post. A comment is a higher level of engagement and a great way to strengthen the connection. There are people who so actively comment, share, and like my posts, they are now familiar to me. (Thanks, Shawn and Darlene!) A few words of caution with updates: remember that this is a professional platform. LinkedIn is not the place to post personal content on a regular basis. Occasionally sharing something personal like a photo or experience is fine. As with any social platform, don't overdo it. Be active, have a presence, but don't post multiple times a day. A few times a week is typically more than enough.

Group Communications

I'm a huge fan of LinkedIn groups. You can join many groups, but it is not realistic to be active in every group you are a member of. Don't be afraid to join a group even if you don't plan to read every post. Groups expand the people who can find and connect to you easily. They also show your interests and give others a place of common interest to start a conversation. I categorize my group activity level into four types:

1. **Actively Engaged.** To be actively engaged, post in the group, ask questions, "like" content, and comment on updates. One of the best ways to actively engage is to answer questions posted by other members. This shows your desire to contribute in a greater way to the community.

2. **Monitor Content.** To monitor content, select the frequency of notifications you want from the group. I usually choose weekly so the content is still fresh. That way I can read the articles of interest and manage my email volume. You can select to follow a specific conversation as well.

3. **Visit as Needed.** You can opt out of notifications and instead occasionally visit the group to scan activity. It may also be a group that is only relevant at times or one you want to share content with. Don't over-post in a group. Ensure your posts are of value and interest to the members.

4. **Moderate.** When you moderate a group, you set the rules about what is appropriate to post and what is not. You can approve comments or allow anyone to post. The level of activity in the group can be left to chance, or you can post with a set level of

frequency. Early on I started my own LinkedIn group called CTC (Coaches, Trainers, & Consultants) Connections.[1] It was an invite-only group of people I met in the industry. We posted questions, shared resources, and even formed offline collaborations. When people started to ask to join, I realized the concept was of interest to a larger audience. So I created an open group and made a subgroup of the founder's circle. My colleague, Arnaldo Carrera, founded a LinkedIn group called ConnectorsClub,[2] which inspired this book.

Notifications and Privacy Settings

One of my favorite ways to leverage LinkedIn is through notifications. You can select the frequency and type of notifications you receive and from whom (first connections, group members, etc.). Notifications have several benefits. First, a notification keeps you up to date on what is happening with your connections: new jobs, birthdays, profile updates. This gives you reasons to drop a quick message and stay in someone's mind (without getting in their face).

I don't recommend using the feature that posts an automatic congratulations. People get the exact same wording from dozens of people; it feels rote. Take the time to personalize the note. It takes three seconds to write, "Congratulations on your new role! What are you doing? How do you like it?" People notice; it feels much friendlier than a simple touch of a button and invites an extension of the conversation. Repeat after me: *personalize, personalize, personalize.*

LinkedIn tells you how many people have viewed your profile. The number is an indication of the effectiveness and searchability of your profile. In the paid version, you can see exactly who viewed your profile, a feature I miss in the free version. You can see a few names as well as the top titles and companies that viewed your profile. I find it interesting to learn what keywords were used to find my profile. All of this helps enhance your profile. I have been known to reach out to someone who viewed my profile and connect.

Another feature of notifications is to have your name pop up in your network's feed. Be careful with your privacy settings especially when you are working on your profile. You don't want an update blasted to your network every time you edit a portion of your profile. Turn the "Update Your Network" setting on and off with major updates.

Curate or Create Content

A last option for engaging is to create or curate content. Creating content includes posting videos, articles, or questions that create a conversation or an exchange of ideas or resources. If you blog, share the blog on LinkedIn to expand your reach. Not everyone wants to write their own content, and you don't have to! I find it can be just as effective to curate and distribute content, sharing the articles that matter most to you. You can build relationships with leaders in your field by using your platform to amplify their content. Sharing the hard work of others elevates you, and it feels good. Show that you actually read the article you are posting with a personal comment such as, "I loved this article, and though I disagree with number four, I think number one is spot on." You may even add, "Which is your favorite?" to inspire and invite others to comment and engage.

How to Leverage LinkedIn for Business Development

Why did I choose Dennis Brown (AskDennisBrown.com) as the expert for this topic? He went from $0 to more than $20 million in sales by leveraging LinkedIn and social selling. I was mesmerized hearing his story from his first sales job in college to selling his multi-million-dollar business.

According to Dennis, "I was the worst sales guy they had ever hired. I was terrible. Probably because I lacked confidence and was awkwardly introverted. I fumbled and I stumbled every step of the way. I was so nervous I almost quit daily during my first couple months." As his confidence grew, so did his results: by the end of his first year, he was one of the top salespeople.

After six months, he left the financially failing company thinking he could do it himself… only to struggle for years. In 2003, with no experience or industry background, Dennis started a third-party logistics company. As he puts it, "We provided freight management services to manufacturers and distributors. Basically it was like owning a trucking company without any trucks."

This is when it got interesting. Dennis was generating leads online through content marketing but was a total naysayer when it came to social media. His Facebook account was under the alias "James Bond." When he stumbled across LinkedIn, he decided "to give it a try for a few months to prove that I was right and social media for B2B was nothing more than BS."

Within a couple months of signing up, he landed a client. A six-figure client that would go on to do close to $1 million in sales with him over the next few years. A new believer, Dennis created a LinkedIn marketing system, which became his primary way of generating new business. From 2008 to 2013, his company generated more than $20 million in new business, most of which was annual recurring revenue.

After using LinkedIn to reach more than $80 million in sales, Dennis sold the business. Now he helps clients around the world generate more leads and sales through LinkedIn and social selling. We developed these seven tips based on his three Cs approach:

1. **Create.** Design a compelling profile focused exclusively on your target market.

2. **Connect.** Profile, find, and connect with your target market.

3. **Convert.** Engage and convert prospects into an offline meeting.

Seven Tips to Leverage LinkedIn for Business Development

1. **Define Your Exact Target Market.** You can't sell unless someone wants to buy. Who needs your offering? As Dennis puts it, "It is virtually impossible to hit the target without first being able to see it." He suggests you "take one sheet of paper and start writing

down your exact target market. Consider industry, geography, job titles, internal divisions, company size, etc." Branding expert Maria Ross suggests you create an avatar, or persona, of your ideal customer. She explains, "You have to know your ideal customer intimately or you will never be able to serve them." Name your avatar, give them a specific age and lifestyle. Maria wants you to "be as specific as possible to create one real person. Think about what their life is like from hobbies to fears to causes."

2. **Optimize Your Profile.** Dennis warns you not to treat your profile like a résumé: "Treat it like a personal branding website that is designed to speak to your exact target market." A few key areas to tweak:

- **Photo:** Wear attire that reflects what you want to reflect—a suit if you're working in a banking field, or a hip T-shirt if you're going for jobs in a creative field such as music, graphic design, or even at a start-up. I always recommend choosing a colorful top or tie as it helps you stand out. I believe in a smile, but you have to be comfortable—you have to be *you*. Think about what the photo says about your brand. I am fine with the outdoor shot if it is related to your work. LinkedIn is a professional platform.

- **Headline:** "Your headline should not be your job title," advises Dennis. Instead he wants you to "focus on the value you can provide your target market." His is a great example of that stating, "Over $20 Million w/ LinkedIn & Social Selling Ask Me How?" I have changed mine so many times trying to implement this advice!

- **Summary:** I have received many tips about writing a compelling summary and have received both positive and less than glowing feedback about mine. My favorite advice was to write in the first person. I believe a conversational tone starts the connection unlike those that read like a bio in the third person. Dennis wisely recommends "formatting in short one to two sentence paragraphs with bullet points so it's easy to consume." A key point in the age of mobile consumption. To keep your profile fresh, include what you are currently working on. For example, when I was writing this book my profile included, "In 2019, I am releasing my fourth book, *The Connector's Advantage.*" You can also include multimedia such as video or SlideShare resentations to your summary and experience sections, which are a differentiating factor.

- **Interests:** I know I just said it is a professional platform, but that doesn't mean you can't explore and show hobbies, interests, or nonprofessional groups. Remember the Laws of Similarity and Association: we connect based on commonalities. A great conversation starter can be about the influencer you both follow or the charitable sector you both support.

3. **Leverage Sales Intelligence.** There is a wealth of information in a person's profile that can be used to build rapport. Dennis urges you to take one or two minutes to learn more about your prospect. Review details about their work experience; the schools they attended; content they post and engage with; influencers and companies they follow; where they are from, live now, or worked in the past; and any common connections or groups. Any one of these areas can create a conversation starter that builds connection.

4. **Use Social Proof to Amplify Your Message.** When Dennis said, "When you say it about yourself, it's bragging. When someone else says it about you, it's proof," it resonated with me. Historically, it has been harder for women to self-promote, but it is not easy for anyone. So let someone else do it for you. After every talk, I reach out to people asking for a testimonial or recommendation on LinkedIn. I find that people will endorse my skills (without a request) thanks to LinkedIn prompts. People look at the number of recommendations and endorsements as an indicator. What do you want it to indicate about you?

5. **Create Engaging LinkedIn Content.** Dennis believes this is by far the best way to become known, build a tribe, and position yourself

as a valuable resource to your clients as an expert in your niche. The two main ways to create content on LinkedIn are updates and articles. Updates on LinkedIn are intended for short-form information and can include a video or image along with up to 1,300 characters. Depending on your privacy settings, your post will be spread to some of your first- and second-degree connections. The main difference with articles is the length and accessibility. You can have up to 40,000 characters in an article and they are easier to access. Finding an old update can be a slog since there are typically more to weed through. With either updates or articles, you can include an image, video, or audio file. There are varying opinions on the frequency of posting. Dennis teaches you to "post once a day or at least two to three times per week." He is not a fan of any posting automation tools like Hootsuite or Buffer because, as he shares, "in my experience it will limit your reach and get less engagement." My feeling is mix it up between automated and live posts.

6. **Focus on Relationships, Not Transactions.** Don't propose on the first date. As Ivan Misner, founder of BNI, says, "Don't be guilty of premature solicitation." You do not ask for a referral or for business too early in the relationship. Dennis warns, "You are selling to the most educated buyers in history with easy access to vast amounts of information about your company, products, and your competitors." Ivan's article title, "When It Comes to Networking, Farmers Will Always Beat Hunters," is a great analogy. It is not about one-shot meetings. It's about cultivating relationships—planting the seeds for future harvesting.

7. **Be Patient.** I love that this is a key tip from Dennis and ties right back to the Law of Patience: give it time, things happen. Rome wasn't built in a day and neither are lasting relationships. Be patient and take your time. Dennis reminds us, "LinkedIn and social selling is not a cure-all. It is a part of a bigger sales and marketing process when done right."

More Virtual Connecting Platforms:
Facebook, Twitter, Instagram, Snapchat, Pinterest...

The abundance of social media platforms is partly thanks to social media being one of the easiest ways to build broad connections. To create a true connection, seek to transfer the virtual relationship offline. To show your interest and support of a virtual connection, like, share, or comment on their activity. As I said before, don't just connect to them, engage with them.

Social platforms give you the ability to connect with those you may not encounter in your everyday, especially with those who are more established. Beyond the basics, you can blog about their work or create a "best of" list post on a specific topic and include many connections you admire. When sharing their content, be sure to tag them so your name appears in their notifications. Seeing your name supporting their posts will create a positive association and name recognition. Some may even follow you back, as often happened for my editor, who met many of her future clients on social media.

It's easy to get overwhelmed by the myriad of ever-changing social media options. My advice is to pick two or three platforms that are best for your particular industry, and focus your attention there. Ask yourself, "What platform do the people I want to connect with use?" One important tip for all: saying something online is no different than saying it in person—except online, what you say can go viral. So remember that what you do on social media platforms impacts how people perceive you. Your social media presence can also positively or negatively impact your job search. A Career Builder study determined 70% of employers use social media to research candidates before hiring; 54% of employers have found content on social media that caused them not to hire a candidate for an open role.[3]

Here are a few currently popular platforms other than LinkedIn. I have accounts on all but Snapchat, but I am only truly active on two.

Facebook

Facebook was originally created for college students and has evolved to all age groups. Businesses also create pages to enable communication with consumers. It is currently the world's largest social network based on number of active users, though the demographic of the user base is aging. The largest growing sector is those 55 and over. The official purpose of Facebook is to make the world more open and connected and that it does, sometimes with oversharing. Consider limiting your frequency of posts and be mindful of volatile topics and going on personal tirades.

Twitter

Twitter is a microblogging site best for sharing news, commenting on current events, or pushing a movement forward in real time. Through hashtags, you can follow a trending topic and add to a larger conversation. It is a global platform and enables connection that may not occur on other social sites. Twitter provides a stream of quick updates from friends, family, academics, politicians, news journalists, and experts. It empowers people to become amateur journalists of life, writing in 280 characters or less about something that they found interesting. It is an easy platform for consumption of information and amplifying messages posted by people you follow.

Instagram

Instagram is a photo-sharing application that allows users to share pictures and videos publicly or to preapproved followers from a smartphone. Celebrities and style icons flock to Instagram for its image-editing tools and comment features, which provide instant feedback from followers. Some of the most-followed brands share eye-popping images (just take a look at *National Geographic*'s @natgeo account) and are finding significantly more influence and engagement here than on other social media platforms.

Snapchat

Snapchat was originally focused on private, person-to-person photo sharing; the photo, or "snap," only played for a few seconds and then it would disappear for good. Snapchat is very different these days. You can now send short videos, live-video chat, message, create avatars, and share photos and videos via a chronological "story" that's broadcasted to all your followers. It is constantly adding features. According to my niece, Snapchat is fun, and people use it to stay in touch and share their lives with one another. She did warn me against letting my preteen get the app after accepting a friend request from someone she didn't know and receiving an inappropriate picture moments later. Famous for its filters that will make you look like a puppy or swap faces with a friend, Snapchat is a hit with the teen population.

Pinterest

Pinterest is a social network that allows users to visually share and discover new interests by posting images and videos—known as pins—through collections known as pinboards. The site is focused on the concept of a person's lifestyle, allowing you to share your tastes and interests with others and discover those of like-minded people. The social network's goal is to "connect everyone in the world through the 'things' they find interesting." Its membership is predominantly female. This social media platform is best for visual industries, such as decor, fashion, makeup, and food. If your career or hobby is not related to a visual industry, this platform may not be worth your time.

Manage Your Contacts with a CRM

In 2015, I was honored to be named one of *Forbes'* top 25 networking experts. So what do people named networking experts do? They start reaching out to each other, of course! That is how I connected with Zvi Band, a relationship marketing pro who cofounded a customer relationship management (CRM) tool called Contactually (Contactually.com).

I have to be honest: I have never used a CRM. I thought those tools were for salespeople or real estate professionals. They seemed overly complex, and maybe in the past they were. In the simplest terms, a

CRM is a database. Zvi opened my eyes to how everyone can benefit from having a system to, as he put it, "help you stay engaged with the relationships that matter to your business and your career." Nowadays, these intelligent databases can do so much data aggregation that they make staying connected easier.

The truth is, any systematic approach is better than none. You can use an Excel spreadsheet, Outlook, or any tool designed to do some of the heavy lifting for you. Whatever your method, Zvi explains that "you have to start off by capturing everyone you know. Your CRM should track everything you do. Many systems actually pull in your email conversations, calendar events, Excel spreadsheets, and phone contacts and can even track most phone calls and text messages." Zvi shared three things any CRM should do for you.

1. **Make Your Life Easier.** Your database should be a digital representation of the real world. A CRM can show you your last conversations, notes from you and your team, and Contactually even includes data found online about your contact. According to Zvi, "A CRM has tools that help you prioritize the relationships that will make the most impact." Your database should tell you who to talk to and when to talk to them.

2. **Provide Intelligence That You Wouldn't Otherwise Have.** I read an article about Contactually's Best Time to Email tool. I asked Zvi how it increased users' responses by 20%. He explains, "This is achieved by continuously analyzing the relationships between users and their networks." Contactually will show you the exact best time of day to reach out, because it is tracking when your communications are getting opened, clicked, and replied to. Different systems have different types of intelligence about your contacts.

3. **Help You Engage.** I have asked thousands of audiences why they don't follow up. One of the most common responses is, "I have nothing to say" or "I don't have a reason to." Telling you who to engage with is only one piece of the puzzle. The content of the

reach-out is another. A CRM can make the reach-out quick and efficient. Zvi explains the ability to "help users follow up with someone by leveraging email templates, pre-built campaigns, and insights you wouldn't otherwise have."

If a CRM can do all of this, it is not just making your life easier and more efficient, it is vastly improving your connectedness. At the end of the day, the best CRM is the one you use. Zvi put is best when he said, "A CRM does a lot of things for you automatically, but your relationships still need you." With whatever tool you use, you have to get into the constant practice of using it. The whole point of a CRM is not just to keep you organized, but to keep you connecting.

The Dos and Don'ts of Digital Connecting

One of the founders of the Authoress group, digital media innovator Sarah Granger (SarahGranger.com), truly knows her stuff when it comes to connecting online—she grew up alongside the internet and has studied the social and technical changes that have occurred during that time. She provides great advice in four major digital dilemmas for succeeding in building online relationships, personally and professionally. Sarah is an award-winning digital media innovator and author of *The Digital Mystique: How the Culture of Connectivity Can Empower Your Life—Online and Off.*

Privacy

I have been unpleasantly surprised when my students had access to photos other people posted of me in my teenage years. I completely agree with Sarah's warning: "Your privacy is vital to consider everywhere, but *especially* on the internet." Sarah suggests that if you're new to online networking, you should begin with your inner circle, your real offline friends. Keep your accounts private until you build a comfort level with the technology and then begin to loosen the reins. She advises, "Don't be afraid to share. If you hold back too much, you'll never find people with whom you share common interests. Show who you are and what you're thinking about, what you're reading, why you're interested, what amuses and frustrates you."

Authenticity

The Law of Authenticity is the first chapter in *The 11 Laws of Likability* and foundational to building any type of relationship. This topic is also aligned with the first mindset of a Connector: to be open and accepting. Sarah believes in revealing your true self online—to an extent. Her advice: "You always want to leave a little bit to yourself, and you want to show the best side of yourself, but within the realm of authenticity. Anyone can smell a fraud on the internet!" As Sarah says, "The more you use your own unique voice online, the better it will shine through and build a network and an audience for you." One thing she warns you not to do is fluff yourself up as an expert. Instead, let others figure it out. As she puts it, "The more you share about your work, your passions, your thoughts and insights, the more your expertise on the topics that matter to you will become clear. If you try to shove it down people's throats by oversharing, being redundant, or spamming, you'll lose the trust of your network."

What to Share

This is probably the most common question or concern: "What should I post and what shouldn't I post?" It is vital to control your content and what is out there about you. I actually google myself and audit the images to make sure there are no unfavorable pictures. A good thing for anyone to do, especially if you are job searching. According to Sarah, the more information you put out there about yourself and your work, the more control you have over the image you present of yourself and the message you deliver to the world. She emphasizes, "The internet is a vast universe of information and the only way to ensure that you don't get lost in it is to keep a strong presence." However, never assume someone knows something just because you posted it online. Everyone is busy and consuming content in varying amounts. I have been surprised many times by information I didn't know because it was only shared on Facebook. Sarah advises, "If there's something important going on that you're excited about or that you feel your network should be aware of, let them know about it." Share your news. That's what social media is for.

Build Relationships

Just as in person, connecting online has a defined etiquette. It is important to take time to get to know people. Sarah asserts it is very possible to meet online and then develop a real relationship. Generally, the relationship progression is "you connect through another person or on a social network, exchange a few comments, maybe becoming 'friends.' Then you learn more about each other, follow up with further discussion, conversing in private messages or email. Once you realize you have something more complex to talk about, you start texting or planning Skype chats." From there, you can develop a real friendship. But she's careful to warn, as others have too, that you shouldn't immediately ask for something. It happens constantly: "Someone will send a cold email asking for a favor, only providing a very brief introduction as to why they might be worthy of your help. Occasionally this is fine, if it's pitched professionally in an environment where pitches are requested, or if it's done through a mutual introduction and requires very little of the recipient's time." Sarah and I are in complete agreement that you should first build a relationship before you ask for assistance. And always remember that connecting is just the first step. Maintaining connection requires consistent dedication.

YOU DO not have to nor should you use every tip mentioned in this chapter. The ideas for engaging virtually and leveraging technology to strengthen relationships are a jumping-off point to pick and choose from. Find what works for you and your personal schedule and goals. Have your own ideas about who you will connect with and why. Diversify your channels of connections. Keep connecting and watch your relationships expand exponentially.

Refresh
Your Memory

LinkedIn is the social media manifestation of everything I say, teach, and write about connecting with a mission to connect the world's professionals to make them more productive and successful.

Follow or connect. Follow people who you don't seek a full relationship with. Consume their content and amplify their message. Connect with those you want to create a two-way exchange and move from online to offline.

Start a conversation. Don't mistake an accepted connection as a real connection. Look at their profile for commonalities and extend the relationship. Don't just click accept; start a conversation.

Engage. Create or curate content. Creating content includes videos, articles, or posing questions that create a conversation or an exchange of ideas or resources. Like, share, or comment on others' posts to engage.

Optimize your profile. Your profile should be more than a résumé. Think of it as an introduction and a reflection of your personal brand. Design it to speak to your target market.

Leverage sales intelligence. There is a wealth of information in a person's profile that can be used to build rapport. Take a couple of minutes to learn about each prospect.

Focus on relationships, not transactions. Take a long-term approach. Don't ask for a favor, referral, or business too early in the relationship.

Leverage tech. Try a customer relationship management (CRM) tool to create a database of your connections and conversations. It may help you stay in touch and in mind.

12

Diversify Your Connections and Stay Connected

"Strive not to be a success, but rather to be of value."

ALBERT EINSTEIN

THE PREVIOUS chapter talked about expanding the way you connect by considering different platforms, channels, and technology. Different stages, ages, life events, and career goals may dictate different needs and wants in connecting. This chapter is about staying connected even when circumstances make it more difficult and, more importantly, about connecting with diverse types of people.

Stay Connected

Staying connected is one of the hardest aspects of being a Connector. I think this is partly because Connectors are constantly making new connections and the sheer number of people may make it unrealistic to stay connected to all of them. The other likely cause is simply a change in circumstances. People move, change jobs, kids change schools, and connections get lost in the process. Oftentimes our strongest relationships of the moment are those of convenience, proximity, or need. When connections don't fall into those categories, they can fall off the radar and fade. That is when you have to make a conscious effort to stay connected.

Staying in touch doesn't mean calling someone every week or every month. I have connections that go back over a dozen years and we only talk once or twice a year. It is okay for ties to loosen, just not sever. Choose to reduce your frequency of reach-outs and vary the communication channels you leverage to enable you to maintain contact when circumstances make it more effort than ease. There are two life situations that cause this need to stay connected more so than others: change of job and change of location. Read on for tips to stay in touch when life happens.

How to Keep in Touch from a Distance or When Working Remotely

While I was working on the book, my editor was the perfect sounding board for me. She had just moved from the East Coast to Colorado and was feeling like she would lose her hard-won professional contacts *fast*. She asked, "How do you maintain your network when you are not there anymore?" She is not alone in her predicament. A Gallup poll found the number of employees working remotely in some capacity continues to rise each year, and those employees working remotely spend more time doing so.[1] You only have to look at the meteoric rise of co-working spaces to see that traditional workplaces are changing—and quickly. No longer are employees chained to their desks from nine to five. I am a fan of this newfound flexibility, but along with it comes challenges, including the challenge to stay connected. When you are not on-site or working face-to-face, it is incredibly easy to feel like you are out of the loop and, worse, *lonely* when working remotely.

Working overseas, moving away, or even just working remotely are all common causes of less face-to-face time and increase the need to be intentional about staying connected. We are increasingly living in a world of virtual connections—especially as people crisscross the globe to pursue new jobs and opportunities. Don't think that leaving a city, state, or even country means you can't maintain the connections you've made there—nothing could be further from the truth in today's day and age. Here are three ideas to help you keep in touch.

Leverage Technology

We connect in so many different ways nowadays. My assistant is virtual. She's worked for me for over two years. We connect via Skype once a week and have never met face-to-face yet I feel like she's my little sister. When working remotely, I suggest you leave your instant messaging app or Skype open all day. It makes it easy for that quick conversation when you can't just walk past someone at the watercooler.

It's vital to nurture distance relationships, and technology enables us to keep connections even when we're not physically present. There is a plethora of tools to assist. All the social media platforms have messaging functionality. I often see a name on Facebook and jot a quick a note saying, "I saw you online and just wanted to say hi. How are you?" It's enough to keep friendships you had in middle school alive—you can see each other at a reunion and it will feel like no time has passed. You don't have to have a specific reason to reach out all the time. Try sending an email to say, "You keep popping into my mind, just wanted to reach out and say hello!" That small act can keep that connected feeling going.

Share Your Space

Working remotely and working from home are two different things. Staying connected to those you work with is easily accomplished through technology and the less frequent live exchanges. Combating the feeling of isolation is entirely different. Co-working spaces are a great way to feel like you are still in a work environment without the long commute. When I first moved to the suburbs, there was no co-working space option. I joined a mom-owned business group and we created our own. A few of us would rotate houses with shared Wi-Fi; each of us was highly productive in a different room and a few at a shared table. Natural coffee breaks in the kitchen created the same feel as an office environment. One more thought: get moving. One way not to feel too isolated is to change your scenery. You can try the local coffee shop or simply walk and talk. One way or another, find a reason to leave the house if only to pick up lunch.

Consider Your Timing

Staying connected doesn't mean talking every day or week. Certain relationships can be an annual thing: reach out once a year to check in, make a date to catch up, congratulate them on their new role on LinkedIn, or say happy birthday. Those little correspondences can put you back into someone's mind, and that's really all you need. I think handwritten cards are fabulous, though I rarely do them, because they're not my thing. I would much rather get on the phone with you. What's your preference? Find what works for you. I have friends and family members who send out the annual update about all the goings-on in their life and family. Every year, I throw a Super Bowl party; the invite list is now more than 100 people. If they can't all make it, I am relieved and it still works—my invitation has maintained the connection.

How to Stay Connected When You Are Out of the Workforce

Close to 90% of my cluster in business school got laid off at some point in the early 2000s, myself included. There are many reasons why you may be out of the workforce, whether voluntarily for parental leave or involuntarily from a layoff. There is often a stigma in being unemployed, whether real or in our own mind, that inhibits relationship-building. You may feel you have nothing to offer or worry that your network will feel put upon. If you are connecting and continually thinking about adding value, timing and employment status won't matter. If you are starting your network from scratch, remember the Laws of Likability and Connector mindsets that enable strong relationships to develop. I get it—when I left corporate America to start my own business, I felt detached from my old network, especially since I started a business in a completely unrelated field to my finance career. Meeting up for a drink or lunch with former colleagues, attending in-person networking events, and staying in touch via social media helped me maintain those relationships, which are still a big part of my life today.

Staying connected when out of the workforce is critical if you ever plan to go back—and important even if you don't. Lisen Stromberg, author of *Work PAUSE Thrive* (LisenStromberg.com), has some great tips on how to do just that. The good news is, according to Lisen's research, 89% of women who had left the workforce were able to reenter successfully. If possible, she suggests you keep your break short, fewer than five years. "While 78% of our survey participants who had paused their careers had no regrets, the longer they were out, the more they regretted their decision to pause," Lisen shares. She also suggests volunteering with purpose; to expand your network, choose your causes to connect with people in the field you plan to reenter.

We all know to stay in touch with former colleagues. I suggest staying on top of the industry issues, people, and companies so you are still in the conversation, even if only socially. Lisen advises you to also "stay abreast of the latest technology. Doing so will make your reentry much smoother and help overcome potential biases employers may have about your ability to be immediately productive." One final word of advice from Lisen: "Make the most of your time off, and don't feel guilty about it for a second. Taking the time to pause, however that looks for you, can be the key to a life well lived—one that ensures you thrive both personally and professionally." I extend that thinking to those involuntarily unemployed as well. Circumstances have created the opportunity for you to reevaluate and be intentional about your next move. If you can manage it financially, don't rush yourself.

Diversify Your Connections

Cognitively diverse teams solve problems faster than teams of similarly thinking people, according to research published in the

Harvard Business Review.[2] It is that diversity that fosters a more creative and innovative workplace. However, it is the diversity of your connections and the quality and quantity of those relationships that contributes to your personal innovation and impact. Expanding your connections and being an Inclusive Connector is critical to attaining faster, easier, and better results.

How to Connect with Influencers

Influencers are the people we all dream of connecting with: the powerful, the famous, the CEOs, and entrepreneurs. We want to learn from them, we want to work for them, or maybe we just want to hang out with them. "How I Got Rob Lowe to Play Me on TV" was the title to a blog post by John Corcoran, podcaster and founder of Smart Business Revolution (SmartBusinessRevolution.com). So whom else would I reach out to for advice on connecting with influencers? After all, he is a former White House speech writer. He agreed to provide some tips from his Connect with Influencers course.

Do Your Research. This should go without saying anytime you are reaching out to a new contact. In the past, it may have felt like stalking to know too much before you met someone. Now it is almost insulting if you don't spend a little time to learn about someone. "It's easier than ever to find out about a particular influencer or VIP and what they're interested in—just take a look at their different media platforms," John suggests. Knowing a bit about them can help offer an entrée into a stronger conversation with them.

Think About How You Can Benefit Them. We have already covered the philosophy of first considering how you can help others. This does not guarantee anything but does increase the probability they will help you. "People think they can't possibly deliver anything of value to VIPs, but that's simply not true," says John. I love the example he shares about when White House staffers were invited to meet briefly with President Clinton. "My family flew in and had heard the President had just gotten a DVD player and was a huge fan of old Western movies. So we brought in a few for him to watch and we had a long discussion with him about the genre, because it was something he was passionate about. There we were with the leader of the free world standing in the heart of power, and we got a lot more time with him than the others, simply because we focused on something of interest to him." John believes anyone can add value, for example, "If you are a human resources employee who wants to advance in your career, write a review of the top 15 most respected people in HR, such as people who've written books on the profession or people in top companies you may want to work for. You've just added feathers to the caps of 15 highly influential people in the field and given yourself a reason to reach out to them—that benefits them.

Get Clear on Your Goals. John suggests you "generate a list of 50 people you'd like to deepen a relationship with over the next 12 months, and earmark a few as high priority contacts." He doesn't want you to contact them all right away. "You'll be significantly more successful if you establish consistency over time," explains John. Influencers are constantly getting barraged by requests asking things of them, but it's very rare to hear from one person who follows up consistently—and you can stand out that way. In fact, that's how he managed to get a full-time gig at the White House. John shares, "When I was a White House intern, I stayed in touch with staffers there—sending them article clippings I thought would be useful to them or snippets of a speech. I tried to deliver value to them on a regular basis." It clearly worked since one of his connections called up to say there was a job in Presidential Letters, and he got it.

Find Different Ways to Connect. The reason John wants you to have such a large list of people you'd like to deepen a relationship with is that sometimes, it's not going to work out. You won't always click with influencers in your field and that's okay. Look for opportunities to connect in person. It could be attending a conference they're going to be at, joining a group they belong to, or inviting them to something you're already attending. Another great option is interviews. John has done them for his blog, podcast, and articles he writes for various sites. He says, "The medium matters less than you'd think. Sometimes people think they need to be writing for a big publication or doing a podcast with a ton of downloads, but that's not true. I remember one college student who reached out to the billionaire Mark Cuban for an interview, got it, and then published it on his free WordPress blog."

Extend the Relationships. To extend the relationship, look for opportunities to deliver value to that person. John suggests you "figure it out by asking, 'What do they need right now?' Do they have a book you can help promote, perhaps in your company newsletter or a local publication? Do they need a LinkedIn recommendation or a glowing Amazon review? What is it that's relevant to *them*?" At the end of each of my interviews with the experts that contributed to this book, I always asked what they were working on and what would be helpful to them. Ivan Misner said he was always open to media opportunities so I made a few introductions. I think it made a difference when I asked him to write the foreword, or at least easier for me to ask.

Make the Relationship Benefit You. According to John, "Plenty of people can build relationships, but it's worth taking that next step of turning it into something that can help your career." You have to put yourself out there and he offers a tool he calls the Minimum Viable Offer, which is "a low barrier-to-entry opportunity for you to establish a working relationship with a certain influencer." He gave the example of a photographer offering to do a headshot for much less than the usual fee. He feels it is important that money exchanges hands; it establishes the business relationship and increases the likelihood they will hire you again in the future. John says, "It's important to ask—because if you don't, your business suffers. At some point in the journey of building relationships, you have to go for it—otherwise, what's the point?"

How Millennials Stay Connected

I am aware that times change and the way I think of connecting as a Generation Xer may not be the way of the next generation. We all need to be aware of the differences in how each generation connects. Millennials have surpassed baby boomers and are now America's most populous living generation. I reached out to three connected millennials for advice on how millennials connect, what they could do if they feel unconnected, and what the most successful millennials are doing right. My expert panel included Darrah Brustein, founder of Network Under 40; Beri Meric, founder of Ivy; and Jared Kleinert, TEDx speaker and founder of 3 Billion Under 30.

How Millennials Connect

The first thing Darrah said to me is that she doesn't want to speak for all millennials. I respect that. It makes sense since she said everyone does things their own way. One commonality shared was that millennials rely on technology to reach out efficiently and those tech tools are constantly changing. Another key theme was mobility. Millennials connect on the go, from anywhere. Darrah loves to send a quick text or email to someone during her commute or between calls. In her article "How to Nurture Your Network Effectively without Being Annoying," she shared an easy way to personalize your reach-out: send cards. Not unique? With Bond (Bond.co), you can send handwritten notes from your phone or computer in seconds. Send Out Cards (SendOutCards.com) is another custom card site she suggested.

My favorite millennial approach is networking playdates. Millennials don't strive for work–life balance, they seek **work–life integration** where professionals blend what they do personally and professionally in order to make both work. Suggest a meet-up on the tennis court or golf course. Because millennials multitask more than other generations, parents leverage that common bond, scheduling networking playdates with colleagues who have children of a similar age. I admit I have done this too. It allows you to relate on a personal level and simultaneously strengthen the professional connection.

How Millennials Can Get More Connected

If you loved both the social and scholastic aspects of college enough to miss it, you're not alone. Beri Meric missed it so much he cofounded Ivy, the Social University, which is creating collegiate-inspired communities in cities across the globe. "Universities create deep, truly multidimensional bonds on social, intellectual, and professional levels with people," he explains. He shares his perspective that "sometimes how millennials connect is broken, which is why I started Ivy." He has a few ideas for how millennials can get better connected.

- **Get Involved.** The first step is simply to pick an organization, community, or group activity and get involved regularly. Beri made a good point about doing extracurricular activities in high school and college to appear well rounded, thereby increasing your likelihood of acceptance into school or landing that plum job: "Being engaged matters more after you graduate, when most people's default mode is to spend their free time watching Netflix or heading to bars." Integrate yourself with your city by getting involved with an organization that interests you. Since the average tenure at work nowadays is two years, Beri explains, "Work no longer gives us the sense of identity and belonging it used to. We are social animals that thrive on being engaged."

- **Step Up.** There is a saying that you have to travel the world or read lots of books to expand your horizons—advice I am personally a fan of. However, reading a book by yourself and traveling alone lacks the community aspect. Belonging to a tribe is a critical thing. Beri urges people to take a leadership role and become actively involved in an activity or group you care about, saying, "It's critical that you not only commit and attend on a repeat basis, but volunteer for a position with some meaning. Passive participation is not going to change your life."

- **Make a Commitment.** Cultivating relationships is a long-term effort. Beri agrees, saying, "You can't volunteer once and build lasting contacts. Relationships don't just happen. It requires repeat interactions, and that requires commitment." At the end of the day, you get out what you put in. Beri believes you can have that well-rounded social life by simply engaging. As he put it, "Social media feeds only show people you have added or celebrities you're never going to hang out with, so you need to make an effort to build personal bonds and real relationships."

What the Most Successful Millennials Do Right

Let's be honest, the millennial label comes with a ton of connotations especially from those of older generations. Millennials get a bad rep for being tethered to their technology, unresponsive, entitled, and a slew of other pejoratives. Jared Kleinert, my example of a Super Connector in chapter 3, interviewed the most successful millennials when writing his books. He learned what the outliers do right and why they don't deserve their reputation. Here are five connection success activities he learned along the way.

1. **Write Cold Emails.** Jared found his illustrious mentor, David Hassell, simply by cold contacting him through LinkedIn—and three months later, Hassell responded. Eventually, he brought Jared in as an intern, then offered him a paid position. "You want to utilize the subject line in a very meaningful way, one that leverages social proof," Jared advises. I always suggest referencing a person you have in common if there is one. The word "quick" in the subject also disarms and invites a fast scan of your note. Other keys to a cold email are personalization, seeking to immediately be valuable to them, and Jared emphasizes "a clear call to action that makes it easy for them." Making it easy increases your odds of moving the relationship forward.

2. **Start with Ideal Clients.** "Work with impressive clients as much as possible, and your profile will grow," says Jared, who always seeks to connect with high integrity people. It was his free mentorship exchange with Hassell that led to his being selected to attend the Thiel Foundation's summit celebrating their 20 Under 20 program, which led to a host of other connections. As I have repeatedly said, *connections beget connections.*

3. **Find Mentors at All Levels.** Jared seeks out successful mentors that he admires but also finds that peer mentors are incredibly valuable. I can attest to this having had the same "buddy coach" for eight years. "A great by-product of my books is networking with talented people close to my own age," he shares. "They're experiencing all this with you, one step ahead or behind."

4. **Have High Quality Conversations.** Quality conversations don't have to be long conversations. He suggests talking 30% of the time and listening 70% of the time, and always asking open-ended questions that lead to great conversations. "I'll be vulnerable and share what I'm going through, and also think about how I can be valuable to them," explains Jared.

5. **Build a Following.** Media influence is becoming more democratized than ever before, according to Jared. You can build a following on social media, through an email blast, or even with a podcast, and it won't cost much. "Share your wins and ideas and resources and practices," he suggests. "Start putting yourself out there, and soon you'll be collaborating and cross-pollinating, even with your competition." This tip applies as much to traditional employees as to the freelance and entrepreneurial communities. When employers are filling a position, an online search is at the start of any vetting process.

How to Be an Inclusive Connector

We are in a time in history where showing respect for diversity and cultural awareness is a priority. As a result, there's an increased sensitivity to what we say and an emphasis on political correctness. I believe most organizations and individuals are navigating with intentions of inclusiveness, though they're often unsure how to execute on that objective.

This section was not part of my original plan for the book. It was the conversations I had and the stories I heard that compelled me to figure out how to help you be an Inclusive Connector. The story that struck me first was in an op-ed piece written by Viola Thompson, the president and CEO of Information Technology Senior Management Forum. She is a Black woman in the male-dominated world of technology.

While attending a conference of minority technology leaders, the participants were introducing themselves and proudly sharing their ethnicity. There was a white woman in attendance and while she waited for her turn to speak, she thought to herself, "What am I doing here? I don't have a similar background as the people in this room." And so, she struggled with what she was going to say. She later shared that for the first time, she understood what it was like being in the minority—the "only one" in the room. That was profound. It was a brief view into what people of color experience every day in corporate America. While the attendees were welcoming to her and she appreciated the extension of kindness toward her, she wondered if she had previously exhibited those same expressions of inclusion to others in similar situations.

When Viola shared this story, I questioned my own actions in those situations. Part of being a Super Connector and a Niche Connector is the breadth and depth of your network. To achieve this level, you must diversify your connections beyond those who fit in the similar-to-me category. The ways in which we are similar are not immediately obvious, but the ways we are different often are. We must push past any discomfort or awkwardness.

I reached out to Robbie Samuels, a transgender man and the author of *Croissants vs. Bagels: Strategic, Effective & Inclusive Networking at Conferences* (CroissantsvsBagels.com), for help on how to be a more Inclusive Connector and together we came up with three tips to create a space where people can show up and share more of their full selves.

Recognize and Embrace the Unicorn Within

We've all had experiences feeling like or being the only one. For me, it was my first day on the trading floor: I was the only woman in sight with the exception of an assistant to the treasurer. It was the 2000s, I was shocked. I stood out on the floor for my gender but also for my size. It felt like there was a height requirement to work there; everyone exceeded six feet, towering over my four-foot-ten.

I was the unicorn, slang for someone who stands out from the crowd. Being a **unicorn** means you are unique to the situation and either look or act differently from the norm. Sometimes standing out can work to your advantage, but it doesn't always feel that way. All the obvious and nonobvious differences about ourselves when we walk into a room flood to the front of our minds. It can be paralyzing *or* you can embrace your inner and outer unicorn.

Sometimes your unicorn can be because of the environment: only minority, only man at a women's conference, only _____ ... fill in your blank. Sometimes it is just part of you. My whole life I have been teased about my size. I admit I had dreams of attending my high school reunion having grown to six feet. There are some things you can't change, and many things you don't want to change. So instead of feeling less than, I got better at cracking the joke before anyone else could. I stopped viewing my size as a detriment and found a way to view it as part of my identity. This goes back to mindset number one: be open and accepting, especially of yourself. We are all unicorns. We can find that uniqueness in ourselves and share it, embrace it. If you want to be an inclusive networker, you need to start by including yourself.

Don't Call Out the Differences, Call Out the Similarities

In order to advance on the spectrum of a Connector, you need to broaden the types of relationships you have. Robbie is passionate about radical inclusion, which he explains as "a mindset of what can I do to let people fully show up and bring more of their full selves into the space so they're not compartmentalizing their identity." One of the most important ways to do this? "Don't call out the differences, call out the similarities." Calling out the difference automatically creates separation.

Due to the Law of Similarity and the similar-to-me bias, we tend to surround ourselves with sameness. As a result, when you expand your circle, all you see are the differences. If upon meeting somebody who could add diversity to your network—different experiences, education, life goals, or demographics—by calling out the difference, you immediately exclude them.

Robbie explains it often seems like an innocuous statement such as, "Wow, you're tall. How tall are you?" or "Your name is so exotic!"

I had a moment of panic since I think those can be great conversation starters. I've often commented on someone's name and said, "That's so beautiful" or asked them to spell it so I can remember it. Robbie eased my fears by explaining that what I was showing was interest and admiration rather than highlighting that it was different and making them feel other. To further help determine when a topic could be perceived as calling out the differences, he suggests, "Ask yourself, did they choose it or is it who they are?" If they chose it, they will likely welcome the topic.

Viola's suggestion is to "be clear on your intention behind stating the difference. Reflect on why you feel compelled to notice the difference." You may be thinking, "I want to relate to you and I recognize the difference, but let's not let it stop us from coming together." If so, great, make sure that is the message they receive, rather than making them excluded. She shares that someone commented to her husband that he was the only male in the office. What they didn't say was that he was the only Black man as well. Calling out the differences implies you are thinking about all the differences and that is just the one you felt comfortable verbalizing.

Have a Host Mindset

There are moments in all of our lives when we don't feel we belong. To be an Inclusive Connector, adopt a host mindset. There is a difference between inviting someone and welcoming them in. Having a host mindset applies to an organization as much as an individual. Viola recalls a partner meeting where spouses and significant others were invited. The activity they had planned for the significant others was a spa day. The assumption was that the partner would be a woman and that she would be interested in a beauty treatment. She advises organizations to avoid such assumptions and instead think about "how you want them to be today and making sure that the activities are appropriate for any gender and all or as many ages, races, or ethnicities that you have invited."

In my chapter of the National Speakers Association, we label newcomers with a gold star and refer to them as VIPs. Existing members see that star and make an extra effort to talk with them and introduce them around. At a recent talk I did, an advanced survey enabled the planners to assign tables based on the charitable sector they support. It immediately gave everyone a jumping-off point for conversation and commonalities. Look for ways to mix different levels and expose people to those they don't typically interact with.

Robbie teaches meeting planners to "be aware of what someone needs that would make the experience easier for them." This idea can be broadly applied even when you aren't the host of the event: you can still take on that role of inclusive networker. Consider how you would want to be welcomed and how can you do that for other people. Look for the lone wolves. The host mindset is about reaching out to those who may not feel included. Watch your body language, physical space, and eye contact; all three can be used to invite others into a group conversation. Leave space for others to physically approach and immediately make room to widen the space and invite them in. Extend eye contact to all people in the group, even those who haven't yet contributed to the conversation. When a break occurs, introduce yourself to the person who joined and then introduce the others as well. If you know the organization or other attendees, ask who they would be interested in meeting and help them make the next connection.

MINDSET MISSION
Flip It to Test It

Kristen Pressner, the global head of human resources for a multi-billion-dollar diagnostics company, gives a different take on being inclusive. It was from her "Are You Biased? I Am" TEDx talk that I learned about her technique of **Flip It to Test It**.[3] Part of the challenge in diversifying our connections is our unconscious bias. **Unconscious bias** happens when our brains make incredibly quick judgments and assessments of people and situations without us consciously realizing. Biases are influenced by our background, cultural environment, and personal experiences. Unconscious bias influences the way we make decisions.

Kristen shares with me that she recognized her bias against women leaders when hiring for an executive role. That confused me, since she is a woman leader. She explains, "Eighteen years of being the sole provider for my family of six isn't enough to overcome the cumulative effect of everything I've been exposed to throughout my life." So to be more inclusive, she suggests, instead of trying to pretend bias doesn't exist, "be aware of every instance where someone is outside the default of the cultural norm and test your bias by flipping it." She explains the purpose of the mindset shift is to try to make conscious decisions.

Flip It to Test It is simply that. Change the outlier aspect that may be causing the bias such as gender, age, race, ethnicity, sexual orientation, or anything else: in your mind, remove that aspect and see if it changes the way you think about that person or that situation. For example, if the interview feedback is that the female candidate is coming off as arrogant in an interview, flip to test it and see if you would have the same feeling if the candidate was a male. Flip It to Test It is in essence a mindfulness technique; it is a way of stopping your unconscious brain from driving in order to let your conscious brain make decisions. The act of stopping and flipping it causes you to be conscious again. I love this approach because it is non-accusatory and puts people in discovery mode. Curiosity is the key to change. The technique has infiltrated my brain and I am finding myself testing my thinking and catching myself more often than I expected.

What's the Point?

I decided to conclude this book by sharing how to be an Inclusive Connector, because that is the crux of the Connector mindset: the joy, curiosity, and interest in building relationships with all kinds of people. Connectors may have a natural way of thinking and acting, or they may have learned these mindsets and behaviors over time. A Connector is simply someone who thinks about the value of connection and prioritizes relationships: making them, strengthening them, supporting them, and recognizing those relationships are there to support them too.

I know that some people reading this book may think, "What's the point?" The truth is, you don't always know the point when you are building relationships, whether you are connecting with someone from another generation, an influencer, or anyone different from you. Diversifying your network expands your thinking, your access to information, and the speed at which you can reach different resources, information, and people. If you want to garner the benefits of being a Connector, keep connecting. Branch out to learn about and learn from those who don't look, sound, speak, or think like you. Connect with those with different interests, education, and experiences. A Connector mentality is one that trusts the process: even if they don't know what those results will be at the outset, a Connector knows that real relationships garner real results.

Refresh
Your Memory

Stay connected. If you work remotely, use technology like Skype and instant messaging to replace watercooler chitchat. Remember not all relationships need high-frequency contact to flourish.

Diversify your connections. Build a network that's inclusive of all levels of colleagues, multiple interests, and various types of people. Doing so will contribute to your individual innovation and impact.

Connect with influencers. Think about how you can be of value to them and look for opportunities to connect in person.

Millennial secrets of success include reaching out to people you'd like to work with. Seek out mentors at all levels—even peers.

Be an Inclusive Connector. Adopt a host mindset; welcome others into the fold. Do not call out differences when interacting with others; instead, focus on your similarities.

Embrace the unicorn in you. We are all different. If you feel like you're the only one like you at an event, welcome it. If you want to be an inclusive networker, start by including yourself.

Conclusion: Putting the Book into Action

"Action is the foundational key to all success."

PABLO PICASSO

"IT'S NOT what you know, it's who you know." That's a saying that we've all heard, but few of us understand the true impact that relationships can have in our lives. Our relationships enable our impact to be greater and our results to happen faster, easier, and better than without those connections. A Connector lives and breathes this philosophy.

At the start of this book, I asked you what you want and what level of Connector you want to be. Now is the time to put the book into action to get you where you want to be. To do that, you need to evaluate the mindsets you currently embody and those you need to adopt to increase your connectedness. Use the chart below to begin your self-evaluation. Rate your current skill level of each mindset on a scale of 1 (low) to 5 (high). Then create your action plan to be the type of Connector that is best for you.

MINDSET	DESCRIPTION	SKILL LEVEL (1–5)
Open and Accepting	You are open and share multiple aspects of yourself with others. You do not put on a front or put up walls. You are willing to be vulnerable. You accept yourself, including your unique charms and work to flex when needed. You accept other people's strengths and flaws the same way.	
Clear Vision	You know what you are working on whether it is your 6-month or 10-year plan. You know what you need to accomplish your goals and are willing to ask for and accept help to make it happen.	
Abundance	You believe there is enough to go around and don't make decisions from a place of fear. You see the opportunity in situations and don't judge yourself in relationship to other people.	
Trust	You believe people are generally trustworthy and are willing to give trust to others. You trust yourself and seek to build the trust of others through being authentic, vulnerable, transparent, and consistent in your interactions.	
Social and Curious	You enjoy the process of building connection and use the format that suits you. You are curious and seek to listen and learn about other people, find points of commonality, and opportunities to add value. You recognize introverts and extroverts both have natural, and very different, strengths in connecting.	
Conscientious	You do what you say you are going to do and communicate updates on commitments to stakeholders. You know when to say no, how to say yes, and you don't commit to something if you can't follow through.	
Generous Spirit	You believe in generosity and recognize that there are many ways to add value. You are aware of the pitfalls of being a zealous Connector and set boundaries to mitigate those risks. You are generous with yourself as well as others.	

Whether it's in your home, your community, or your career, the quality of your relationships will impact your life in multiple ways. The breadth and depth of your network is up to you. There are different types of relationships you may want to consider ensuring exist in your circle.

Champions. People in your organization with a seat at the table are all potential champions. They are decision-makers with the power to impact your promotion, salary, bonus, and work assignments. To be an effective champion, they must believe in, speak up for, and even fight for you. The more champions you have, the more your career will skyrocket.

Cheerleaders. These are peers, friends, and even family who bolster your confidence and encourage you along the way. They give a needed pep talk and believe in you, even if sometimes you don't believe in yourself. We all need cheerleaders to help us through the challenges, risks, and failures and to help us celebrate the successes.

Mentors. A mentor is an experienced and trusted advisor and having one is critical to your professional development. They have the expertise you are seeking to acquire and you can learn from them. Mentors can be in or outside your organization and can provide different types of guidance. The more mentors, the more you learn and grow.

Followers. You can't lead if no one wants to follow you. As you rise in the ranks, it is important to reach back and fill the role others have filled for you along the climb. Followers want to work for you and help you get the best results. Meet the needs of your team; show them you care about them and the things they care about and they will follow the leader.

Sounding Boards. Have many. These are the people you go to discuss your ideas, approach, or plan to get their opinion. They challenge your thinking and help you make more informed decisions. Choose people whose opinions are not identical to each other's to push your thinking and broaden your viewpoint.

Confidants. A confidant is different than a sounding board. They are the people you can vent to, confide in, and with whom you can share your secrets. If you choose someone within the organization that may have perspective on organizational politics, be sure they are trustworthy. An external person may not have the complete picture but can help you release frustrations in a safe way.

Think about the people who are currently filling these roles in your life and where you have gaps. Identify people who could fill those roles and reach out. Consider the ideas put forth in these pages and seek to create a mutually beneficial exchange. If you really want to build a connection, it won't happen in only one interaction.

I LOVE how small the world is. Making it even smaller is what this book is about. We all need relationships and connection in our lives. As I said at the start of this book, the results, success, happiness and contentment that Connectors experience isn't because they have luck, it's because they have connections—and you can too. It may sound counterintuitive, but connecting and networking are two very different things. **Networking is something you do; a Connector is who you are.**

Acknowledgments

THIS IS going to be a very long list! I never know whether to start or end with family, as all things for me start and end with family. I thank my husband, Michael: when I told him I wanted to write another book, he asked in a what-the-hell-are-you-thinking tone, "Why?!" I serenely responded, "I have something I have to share, to say, to teach." He shrugged and said, "That's a good reason." And he supported me every step of the way. To my kids, James and Noah, for showing an interest in my work and being my constant motivation. I am grateful to my extended family for all the love and encouragement with a shout-out to my brother-in-law, Ray Meyers, who shaped the last line of the book. I thank my mother, Margot, for all the golden nuggets over the years; my father, Arthur, for instilling confidence in me, and special thanks to my sister, April Meyers, for continuing to inspire me and be the perfect example of a Connector.

Thank you to my rocks, Abby Katoni and Rebecca Friese Rodskog. The two of you talk me off the ledge, listen to me vent, give me feedback, and encourage me. I appreciate you and am thankful you are in my life. Thanks to Erin Budwick and Maria Ross for their input along the way.

John Katzman, thank you for all the mentor moments, the ideas, and the introductions. Your suggestion during a conversation about the book ignited a spark, and the result is the abundance of experts in this book. Thank you, Malcolm Gladwell, for agreeing to be a part of this book.

I must acknowledge Sarah Granger and Denise Brosseau for starting the amazing Authoress group, for your suggestions and introductions, and for adding your expertise to this book. And thanks to all the people who shared their stories and made introductions to people whether or not they ended up in the book.

Thank you to every expert who shared their time, knowledge, and ideas to make this book exponentially more valuable (in alphabetical order): Ari Horie, Beri Meric, Chad Littlefield, Charles Best, Darrah Brustein, Denise Brosseau, Dennis Brown, Dorie Clark, Elisa Camahort Page, Eric Gorham, Ivan Misner, Jaime Masters, James Carbary, Jared Kleinert, John Corcoran, Jordan Harbinger, Kristen Lamoreaux, Kristen Pressner, Lindsay Johnson, Lisen Stromberg, Marshall Goldsmith, Mary Loverde, Matthew Pollard, Michael Lee Stallard, Rachel O'Meara, Rebecca Friese Rodskog, Robbie Kellman Baxter, Robbie Samuels, Ryan Foland, Sarah Granger, Susan RoAne, Viola Thompson, and Zvi Band.

Thank you, Meeghan Truelove, for introducing me to the fabulous Kathryn O'Shea-Evans whose editorial partnership was invaluable. I loved working with you, KOE. Much appreciation to my list of loyal followers who read my emails, gave feedback on the cover, and especially to the nearly 800 of you who took the survey. Speaking of the survey, thanks must go to Stacy Kessler at Montclair State University for helping select the questions and Trevor Kresofsky for analyzing all the data. Arnaldo Carrera, who trademarked the phrase Connectors Club, thank you for inspiring the idea of this book.

Finally, my thanks and appreciation to the entire production team at Page Two starting with Trena White. I knew at the first conversation you were a connection that would last. Thank you for your partnership, collaboration, and support.

Resources

Books

Ask Powerful Questions by Will Wise
Connection Culture by Michael Lee Stallard
Croissants vs. Bagels by Robbie Samuels
The Digital Mystique by Sarah Granger
The 11 Laws of Likability by Michelle Tillis Lederman
Entrepreneurial You, Reinventing You by Dorie Clark
Frientimacy by Shasta Nelson
Giftology by John Ruhlin
How to Create Your Own Luck by Susan RoAne
How to Work a Room by Susan RoAne
The Membership Economy by Robbie Kellman Baxter
Mindset by Carol Dweck
Pause by Rachael O'Meara
Reinventing You by Dorie Clark
Road Map for Revolutionaries by Elisa Camahort Page
The Secrets of Savvy Networking by Susan RoAne
Stand Out by Dorie Clark
3 Billion Under 30 by Jared Kleinert
The Tipping Point by Malcolm Gladwell
2 Billion Under 20 by Jared Kleinert
What Do I Say Next? by Susan RoAne
Work PAUSE Thrive by Lisen Stromberg

Expert Websites

Chad Littlefield and Will Wise: WeAnd.me
Darrah Brustein: Darrah.co
Denise Brosseau: ThoughtLeadershipLab.com
Dennis Brown: AskDennisBrown.com
Dorie Clark: DorieClark.com
Elisa Camahort Page: ElisaCP.com
John Corcoran: SmartBusinessRevolution.com
Jordan Harbinger: JordanHarbinger.com
Lisen Stromberg: LisenStromberg.com
Marshall Goldsmith: MarshallGoldsmith.com
Mary LoVerde: MaryLoVerde.com
Michael Lee Stallard: MichaelLeeStallard.com
Lindsay Johnson: TheRadicalConnector.com
Robbie Kellman Baxter: PeninsulaStrategies.com
Robbie Samuels: RobbieSamuels.com
Ryan Foland: RyanFoland.com
Sarah Granger: SarahGranger.com
Susan RoAne: SusanRoAne.com

Company and Resource Websites

Alyce: Alyce.com
Bond: Bond.co
Contactually: Contactually.com
Donors Choose: DonorsChoose.org
FutureLeaderNow: FutureLeaderNow.com
Gateway to Innovation: G2IConference.com
Intern Queen: InternQueen.com
Send Out Cards: SendOutCards.com
Women's Startup Lab: WomenStartupLab.com

Podcasts

B2B Growth: B2BGrowthShow.com
Eventual Millionaire: EventualMillionaire.com
The Introvert's Edge: MatthewPollard.com/TheIntrovertsEdge
The Jordan Harbinger Show: JordanHarbinger.com/Podcast
World of Speakers: SpeakerHub.com/SkillCamp

Member Organizations

Business Network International: BNI.com

Coaches, Trainers, and Consultants LinkedIn group: linkedin.com/groups/2980318

ConnectorsClub: linkedin.com/groups/1053417

GirlFriend Circles: GirlFriendCircles.com

Information Technology Senior Management Forum: ITSMFonline.org

Ivy: Ivy.com

Network Under 40: NetworkUnder40.com

Society for Information Management: Simnet.org

Young Entrepreneur Council: YEC.com

Notes

1. Connections Are Critical to Success

1   Nikki Waller, "How Men & Women See the Workplace Differently."
    Wall Street Journal (September 27, 2016): http://graphics.wsj.com
    /how-men-and-women-see-the-workplace-differently/.
2   Peter Economy, "This Person's Help Will Make You 5 Times More
    Likely to Get Promoted," *Inc.* (November 13, 2017): www.inc.com
    /peter-economy/this-persons-help-will-make-you-five-times-more-
    likely-to-get-promoted.html.
3   Lou Adler, "New Survey Reveals 85% of All Jobs Are Filled via Networking,"
    LinkedIn (February 29, 2016): https://www.linkedin.com/pulse
    /new-survey-reveals-85-all-jobs-filled-via-networking-lou-adler/.
4   Lydia Dishman, "How You'll Search for a Job in 2017," *Fast Company*
    (January 10, 2017): https://www.fastcompany.com/3066700/how-
    youll-search-for-a-job-in-2017.
5   Valentina Zarya, "Female Founders Got 2% of Venture Capital Dollars
    in 2017," *Fortune* (January 31, 2018): http://fortune.com/2018/01/31
    /female-founders-venture-capital-2017/.
6   Grace Miller, "38 Referral Marketing Statistics That Will Make You Want
    to Start a RAF Program Tomorrow," *Annex Cloud* (March 3, 2016): https://
    www.annexcloud.com/blog/39-referral-marketing-statistics-that-will-make-
    you-want-to-start-a-raf-program-tomorrow/.
7   Ivan Misner, "What Percentage of Your Business Do You Get from
    Referrals?" IvanMisner.com blog post (August 18, 2008): http://ivanmisner
    .com/what-percentage-of-your-business-do-you-get-from-referrals/.

8   Harvey Deutschendorf, "Why Emotionally Intelligent People Are More Successful," *Fast Company* (June 22, 2015): https://www.fastcompany .com/3047455/why-emotionally-intelligent-people-are-more-successful.

9   Zameena Mejia, "Harvard's Longest Study of Adult Life Reveals How You Can Be Happier and More Successful," CNBC (October 31, 2017): https:// www.cnbc.com/2017/10/31/this-harvard-study-reveals-how-you-can-be-happier-and-more-successful.html.

10 J. Holt-Lunstad, T.F. Robles, and D.A. Sbarra, "Advancing Social Connection as a Public Health Priority in the United States," *The American Psychologist* 72, no. 6 (2017): 517–530. doi:10.1037/amp0000103.

11 Emma M. Seppälä, "Connect to Thrive," *Psychology Today* (August 26, 2012): https://www.psychologytoday.com/us/blog/feeling-it/201208 /connect-thrive.

12 Christine M. Riordan, "We All Need Friends at Work," *Harvard Business Review* (July 3, 2013): https://hbr.org/2013/07/we-all-need-friends-at-work.

13 Gallup, "State of the American Workplace," Gallup.com (February 2017): http://news.gallup.com/reports/178514/state-american-workplace.aspx.

14 Drake Baer, "Harvard Professor Finds that Innovative Ideas Spread Like the Flu; Here's How to Catch Them," *Fast Company* (January 17, 2013): https://www.fastcompany.com/3004829/harvard-professor-finds-innovative-ideas-spread-flu-heres-how-catch-them.

15 Towers Perrin, "Working Today: Understanding What Drives Employee Engagement," Retrieved from http://www.keepem.com/doc_files/Towers _Perrin_Talent_2003%28TheFinal%29.pdf.

16 Robbie Kellman Baxter, "How to Seize the Membership Economy Opportunity to 5x Your Company," *Subscription Growth Podcast* (September 12, 2017): http://robertskrob.com/seize-membership-economy-opportunity-5x-company/.

17 Daniel McCarthy and Peter Fader, "Subscription Businesses Are Booming. Here's How to Value Them," *Harvard Business Review* (December 19, 2017): https://hbr.org/2017/12/subscription-businesses-are-booming-heres-how-to-value-them.

18 Peter Schmidt, "A Major Barrier to Alumni Giving: Graduates' Mistrust," *The Chronicle of Higher Education* (November 6, 2015): https://www .chronicle.com/article/A-Major-Barrier-to-Alumni/234100.

19 Bright Local, "Local Consumer Review Survey," (2017): https://www .brightlocal.com/learn/local-consumer-review-survey/.

20 Grace Miller, "38 Referral Marketing Statistics that Will Make You Want to Start a RAF Program Tomorrow."

21 Amy Edmondson, "Psychological Safety and Learning Behavior in Work Teams," *Administrative Science Quarterly* 44, no. 2 (June 1999): 350.

22 Bruce Temkin and Aimee Lucas, "Employee Engagement Benchmark Study, 2017," Temkin Group Insight Report (March 2017): http://www.temkingroup.com/wp-content/uploads/2017/05/1703_EEBenchmarkStudy17_FINAL.pdf.

3. What Level Connector Are You?

1 Malcolm Gladwell, *The Tipping Point: How Little Things Can Make a Big Difference* (Boston: Little, Brown, 2000), 38.

2 Malcolm Gladwell, *The Tipping Point*, 46.

4. Connectors Are Open and Accepting

1 Scott Hays, "American Express Taps Into the Power of Emotional Intelligence," Workforce.com (July 1, 1999): http://www.workforce.com/1999/07/01/american-express-taps-into-the-power-of-emotional-intelligence/.

2 The Johari Window was first published in the Proceedings of the Western Training Laboratory in Group Development by UCLA Extension Office in 1955. Available here: http://www.mbdi.com/workshoprefmaterials/Johari_Window.pdf.

3 Art Markman, "Do You Know What You Don't Know?" *Harvard Business Review* (May 3, 2012): https://hbr.org/2012/05/discover-what-you-need-to-know.

4 Leonid Rozenblit and Frank Keil, "The Misunderstood Limits of Folk Science: An Illusion of Explanatory Depth," *Cognitive Science* 26, no. 5 (2002): 521–562. doi:10.1207/s15516709cog2605_1.

5 The Ladder of Inference was first put forward by organizational psychologist Chris Argyris and used by Peter Senge in *The Fifth Discipline: The Art and Practice of the Learning Organization* (New York: Doubleday, 1990).

6. Connectors Believe in Abundance

1   Jacob Morgan, "The Top 10 Factors for On-the-Job Employee Happiness," *Forbes* (December 15, 2014): https://www.forbes.com/sites /jacobmorgan/2014/12/15/the-top-10-factors-for-on-the-job-employee-happiness/#33ea87715afa; and Rainer Stack, Carsten von der Linden, Mike Booker, and Andrea Strohmayr, "Decoding Global Talent," The Boston Consulting Group (October 6, 2014): https://www.bcg.com/en-us/publications/2014/people-organization-human-resources-decoding-global-talent.aspx.
2   The Redbooth Team, "Everybody's Working for the Weekend, But When Do You Actually Get Work Done?" Redbooth.com blog (November 15, 2017): https://redbooth.com/blog/your-most-productive-time.

8. Connectors Are Social and Curious

1   Carol Dweck, "What Having a 'Growth Mindset' Actually Means," *Harvard Business Review* (January 13, 2016): https://hbr.org/2016/01 /what-having-a-growth-mindset-actually-means.

9. Connectors Are Conscientious

1   M. Brent Donnellan, Rand D. Conger, and Chalandra M. Bryant, "The Big Five and Enduring Marriages," *Journal of Research in Personality* 38, no. 5 (October 2004): 481–504. Retrieved via Marelisa Fabrega, "19 Ways to Be More Conscientious," *Daring to Live Fully*: https://daringtolivefully.com /how-to-be-more-conscientious.

10. Connectors Have a Generous Spirit

1   JoshPalerLin, "How Does a Homeless Man Spend $100?" YouTube.com video (December 22, 2014): https://youtu.be/AUBTAdI7zuY.
2   Michelle Tillis Lederman, "#365LivingGiving," YouTube.com video (May 4, 2015): https://youtu.be/7P0HLt3N-50.

11. LinkedIn and Technology Tools

1   "CTC (Coaches, Trainers, & Consultants) Connections," LinkedIn group: www.linkedin.com/groups/2980318.

2   "ConnectorsClub," LinkedIn group: www.linkedin.com/groups/1053417.

3   CareerBuilder, "Number of Employers Using Social Media to Screen Candidates at All-Time High, Finds Latest CareerBuilder Study," CareerBuilding press release (June 15, 2017): http://press.careerbuilder .com/2017-06-15-Number-of-Employers-Using-Social-Media-to-Screen-Candidates-at-All-Time-High-Finds-Latest-Career-Builder-Study.

12. Diversify Your Connections and Stay Connected

1   Niraj Chokshi, "Out of the Office: More People Are Working Remotely, Survey Finds," *New York Times* (February 15, 2017): https://www.nytimes .com/2017/02/15/us/remote-workers-work-from-home.html; and Gallup, "State of the American Workplace."

2   Alison Reynolds and David Lewis, "Teams Solve Problems Faster When They're More Cognitively Diverse," *Harvard Business Review* (March 30, 2017): https://hbr.org/2017/03/teams-solve-problems-faster-when-theyre-more-cognitively-diverse.

3   Kristen Pressner, "Are You Biased? I Am," TEDx Talks YouTube.com video (August 30, 2016): https://youtu.be/Bq_xYSOZrgU.

Index